Best Pub Walks
in
North Devon

Dennis Needham

Published by Sigma Leisure – an imprint of
Sigma Press, 1 South Oak Lane, Wilmslow, Cheshire SK9 6AR, England.

British Library Cataloguing in Publication Data
A CIP record for this book is available from the British Library.

ISBN: 1-85058-441-9

Typesetting and Design: Sigma Press, Wilmslow, Cheshire.

Photographs and Cartography: Elizabeth Fowler

Additional photography: Alison Fowler

Historical Photographs: from the author's collection

Cover photograph: The Crown Inn, West Down (at the start of Walk 5)

Printed by: Manchester Free Press

Disclaimer: the information in this book is given in good faith and is believed to be correct at the time of publication. No responsibility is accepted by either the author or publisher for errors or omissions, or for any loss or injury howsoever caused. Only you can judge your own fitness, competence and experience.

For Jill, with love

Preface

Walking in the North Devon area can sometimes appear to be a problem. There are so many roads weaving their way around the county that Public Footpaths are a lot less common than in some counties. That said, the narrow back lanes with their high banks can be very secluded places with only an occasional local user disturbing the peace.

One other highway of great benefit to the walker is the green lane. These are to be found all over the county, and are remnants of the past. When roads were adopted and made up by the Highways Authority, some were left out of the plan as surplus. Locals and farmers did not agree, and continued to use them, a tradition that has continued to this day. The only vehicular traffic you will ever meet on a green lane is likely to be a tractor, and, usually being away from the "touristy" areas of the county, you seldom see visitors.

All the walks in this book are circular, finishing at the starting point. Most – but not all – start at a pub: all visit one or more. Hostelries have been chosen with care to represent a cross-section of the wide variety offered in this most glorious corner of England. Where no car parking details are given, it can be assumed that parking at the pub is adequate, but PLEASE, always ask permission. Where it is not available, alternatives are noted.

Dennis Needham

Contents

Locations of Walks

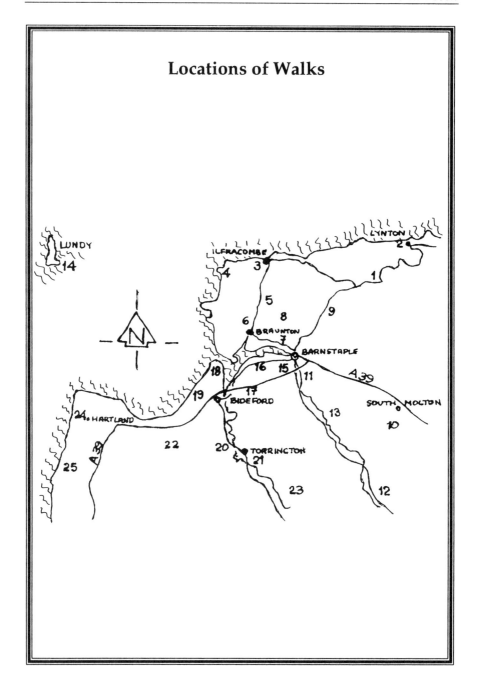

Walk 1:
Parracombe – Churchtown –
Martinhoe Cross – Heddon Valley

The uplands of Devon, within the boundaries of The Exmoor National Park and its superb scenery. A quite magnificent area in which to start your
Best Pub Walks in North Devon.

Distance: 6 miles.

Terrain: Rugged with several hills.

Refreshment: Nothing apart from start/finish.

Map: 180.

Grid Reference: SS 667448.

Starting Point: Fox and Goose Inne, Parracombe.

Transport: Red Bus 310 – Barnstaple to Lynton serves the village. Details on 01271 45444.

The pub is just 100 years old: the present one that is. There has been a public house on this site for centuries, but the last one, a long thatched old building was destroyed by fire sometime between 1892 and 1894. It is remembered by four huge photographs on the wall of the bar.

In addition to a good, reasonably-priced menu, bed and breakfast is available. Liquid sustenance varies with the season. Parracombe has a fair holiday trade, and during the summer, you can always find a guest beer on tap. This can be Boddington's, Castle Eden Ale, Marston's Pedigree, or Flowers IPA. The stock bitter is Flowers, whilst the slightly sweet Addlestones Cider (Gaymers) reminds you that you are in the West Country.

The Lynton and Barnstaple Railway (1)

It's sixty years now since this pretty narrow gauge railway closed, but interest in it is higher than ever. Maybe it's the evocation of times past, perhaps the terrain over which it ran: or just plain nostalgia. Whatever, this nineteen-mile line which ran on a 3ft gauge remains a magnet for rail enthusiasts, and several reincarnations as scale models are seen at exhibitions all over the country.

An undated picture of the Lynton and Barnstaple Railway loco 762 TAW. It was taken between 1927, after the attractive copper-capped chimney was replaced, and 1932 when steam heating was fitted

It was Sir George Newnes, the publisher, who was the prime mover in the establishment of this railway. He lived in Hollerday House, Lynton during the latter part of the nineteenth century, and was Chairman of the company founded to promote construction of the line. An Act of Parliament was passed on June 27th 1895, and work commenced just three months later.

After many trials and tribulations, including the bankruptcy of the main contractor, the line opened on May 11th 1898. It brought instant popularity (and wealth) to Lynton, and the settlement of Lynmouth down on the sea front, linked to Lynton by a cliff railway, also courtesy Sir George. The route ran from Barnstaple Town station up the Yeo valley and out onto the moors towards Bratton Fleming. It took horseshoe curves to reach the wildest parts above Blackmore Gate before Parracombe and the 1,000 ft summit at Woody Bay. Then a gentle descent into the station at Lynton and journey's end. The Rolling stock was quaint – by any standards, and the four locomotives all carried the names of local rivers: Yeo, Taw, Exe and Lyn.

It was never a success commercially. Although the holiday season and

Barnstaple Market on Friday saw heavy loadings, the sparsely populated area could not support it for the rest of the year. It became part of the Southern Railway after the Grouping of 1923, and saw its last passenger service on September 29th 1935. The stock and locomotives were sold, as was some of the track bed. All that is left now are a few fading memories and occasional glimpses of its course. A Preservation Society is hard at work, hoping to re-instate some of the line, but face an uphill struggle: not that it will deter them. Barnstaple Town station still exists, most recently as a tea room and cafe, and the old signal cabin there is run by the Group as a museum of L & B artifacts, together with an outline of their plans.

Narrow Devonian village streets in Parracombe (photo: Elizabeth Fowler)

St. Petrock's Church (2)

This old building has the distinction of being the very first church placed in the care of The Redundant Churches Fund. It was officially declared redundant on November 25th 1969 and taken over by the Fund some twenty months later. An indication of its historical importance is shown by its status as a Grade A Listed Structure.

A place of worship was established on the site in Saxon times, and a church certainly existed at the time of Domesday. The present building is said to have been built by William of Falaise, a relative of William the Conqueror, at the end of the 11th century. The tower was added in 1182, and the chancel in 1252. The main body was rebuilt around the time of Henry VII.

One particularly important aspect of the building is that the interior has remained unaltered for over two hundred years, giving historians – and the interested visitor – a window on village church furnishing and decoration in the 18th century.

Pride of place inside goes to the screen separating the nave from the chancel. The woodwork itself is no more than pleasing to the eye. But the decoration sets it apart. Beautifully painted, it has The Lord's Prayer, The Ten Commandments and The Apostles' Creed, with the Royal Arms occupying the tympanum.

It was as long ago as 1879 that the stability of St. Petrock's started giving cause for concern. Demolition was proposed, but this caused an outcry from around the country as well as locally. Funds were raised for its retention, whilst construction of a new place of worship was soon under way. This became Christ Church, and regular services at St. Petrock's were ended.

Special events continued to be celebrated, albeit with the building in an increasingly dangerous condition. Lightning struck the tower in 1908, and there was storm damage in the winter of 1946/7. Repairs were effected, but the fundamental instability not addressed. In 1969, the south aisle roof needed shoring up to prevent collapse, and general remedial work was placed in hand, funded largely from donations. In 1982, extensive structural work was carried out in an effort to maintain the integrity of the place, and currently, the church is holding together well, offering delight and peace to the visitors who still flock through the door: St. Petrock's is one of the most visited redundant churches in the country.

The graveyard continued to be used for burials until 1971, and is still intact, as are two cottages on the edge of the grounds. Although now in private hands, converted to attractive homes, they were once attached to the church and used as a place to brew the church ale to refresh worshippers.

It is perhaps fitting that such a glorious building was the very first church vested in the Redundant Churches Fund. This was established under Part III of the Pastoral Measures 1968, to preserve churches – or even parts – no longer required for worship. A Pastoral Measure, incidentally, is ecclesiastical legislation passed by the General Synod of the Church of England, ratified by Parliament, and given Royal Assent. It is law, carrying the same legal status as an Act of Parliament.

The Walk

Leave the pub and turn left. After a few yards, a pretty bridge crosses the river Heddon and leads past old stone and cob cottages to a right turn by a telephone box. Take this and walk uphill, past All Saints Church (3). Follow an increasingly narrow lane until it makes a sharp right-hand turn. This was a bridge over the Lynton and Barnstaple Railway (1), while straight ahead is a house with an attractive garden and a model railway that actually uses the bed of the L & B. The garden and railway are open to visitors during the season.

Just beyond the bridge on the left is St. Petrock's church (2) and the tarmac gives way to a rutted track before reaching the busy A39 trunk road. Take the track directly opposite which continues uphill for about 200 yards before bearing to the right and a parting of the ways. Take the Waymarked path to the left which soon veers right to avoid a farm, and into a clearly marked track through two gates and continually uphill.

At the top of the climb is a narrow lane. Turn left. Here, you have reached some 1,000ft above sea level, the highest point on the walk. Some indication of the climb can be gained from the fact that Parracombe is on the 500ft contour. All that notwithstanding, none of the climb is really steep.

Walk along the lane for some 300 yards, and take the right fork which, almost 1 mile later reaches the A39 again at Martinhoe Cross. As you walk along the first half mile or so, take time out to marvel at the views from here. They are simply stunning.

Cross the A39, slightly to the left, and another lane leads away from the main road. Some 1,000 yards along, a gateway on the left gives access to the next section. This is a bridleway signposted Kemacott and Killington. Follow the track around to the right, and then back to the left, keeping fairly close to the hedge on the left. Through gates and stiles, you will drop down into the farm settlement of Kemacott.

Take the gate (waymarked) to the left which leads into a track that soon peters out. Stay more or less on the contour, through a gate and to the edge of a wood. Another gate, and the path then moves downhill and arrives in a narrow lane where a left turn starts off quite steeply uphill again.

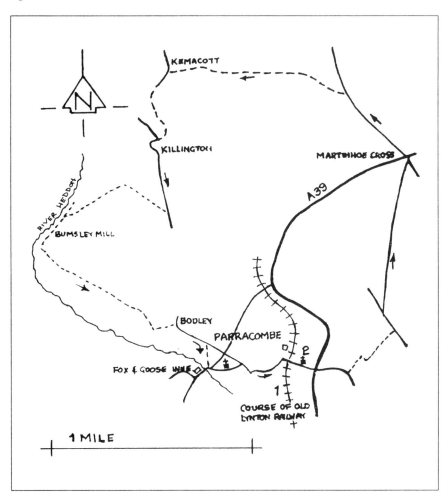

About 500 yards later, as the incline eases a little, a Public Footpath sign points through a gate on the right. Keep close to the fence on the right, and you will pass through another gateway. By sticking to the fence again, you will walk right round the steep hill to your left and at the far side reach a stile. Over this, the path descends very steeply into the Heddon valley and Bumsley Mill.

Almost reaching the river, turn left and follow the track around to the left. This soon becomes less obvious, but a stile and fingerpost point the way forward; onward – and inevitably upward. Over this stile the path moves to the right-hand hedge. Keep close to this for the next quarter of a mile before entering a small field though a gate. The exit is in the far right-hand side.

Eventually, this leads to a paved surface at the settlement of Bodley where a right turn is taken. After 200 yards, a row of houses line the right-hand side, set down below the road a little. At the end of these is a Public Footpath on the right to Parracombe. But please be careful. The somewhat careless location of this post can easily take you down a private drive alongside, and make you very unpopular with the owner.

The path picks its way downhill between houses into the centre of the village, opposite the road up to the church. Bear slightly to the right and the Fox and Goose Inne.

Walk 2:
Lynton – Valley of The Rocks

Parking in Lynton is appalling. For that reason, the rules are varied. A large car park exists halfway along the walk, and it is to there that we gravitate. When the walk reaches Lynton, there are a number of pubs in the town.

Distance: 3 miles.

Terrain: Mainly level, but one steep hill.

Refreshment: Lynton only.

Map: 180.

Grid Reference: SS 708498

Starting Point: Valley of the Rocks Car Park, west of the town.

Transport: Buses to Barnstaple and Taunton. Tiverton and Exeter on Saturdays only.

For this walk, there is no recommended pub. On reaching Lynton, the choice is good, and a short diversion into Queens Street gives access to The Queens, The Globe, and The Crown. They all serve real ale, they all offer food, and they all have a good feel to them. Fence-sitting is required here: make your own choice.

Lynton

The town has been settled for centuries now, but because of its isolation, the more turbulent periods of our history have largely passed it by: Exmoor was a formidable barrier until relatively recent times. The Celts were here long after the Saxons had taken over elsewhere, although Domesday did find it, locating a population of around 400. Seven hundred years later, it had risen; to 481. The Civil War left the place untouched, and it was not until the coming of roads and railways that it began to develop. New houses and hotels were built to accommodate an influx of Victorian visitors.

The publisher Sir George Newnes lived at Hollerday House. A great public benefactor, Sir George was involved in promotion of The Lynton and Barnstaple Railway (see Walk 1), funded construction of the town

The Lynmouth Cliff Railway

hall and also the cliff railway (2), linking the town with Lynmouth. This opened on Easter Monday 1890, costing £8,000. The two coaches are operated by gravity. A tank under the top one is filled with 500 gallons of water from the bottom one. The journey time is under two minutes, with 900ft of track at a gradient of 1 in 1.75.

Intriguingly, in the first two decades of this century when motor cars were not powerful enough to tackle the gradients in Lynmouth, they used the railway. The body of the coach was removed, the car driven onto the platform and lashed down. A one-way trip cost the then-staggering sum of 10/6d (52½p).

Valley of The Rocks

This area is claimed to have once been a centre for Druidism in north Devon. There were great circles of stones, but centuries of vandalism have seen these either removed or destroyed. It is also immortalised in fiction. John Ridd, a character in R.D. Blackmore's story of Exmoor life "Lorna Doone" visited here in the book.

Castle Rock (1)

Stands a sheer 480ft above sea level, and is very popular with climbers. In the summit is a hole known as the White Lady. Local legend has it that the lady lived at the time of the Crusaders and was badly treated by the Black Abbot of Lynton. After her death, a ghost returned to haunt him.

A wild woman called Aggie Norman once lived in a hovel by the rock, and the character of Mother Meldrum in "Lorna Doone" is thought to have been based on her.

The Lynmouth Disaster 1952

It was late on Friday night, August 15th 1952 that the name "Lynmouth" grabbed national headlines as flooding devastated the village. It had been a particularly wet month, with Exmoor very soggy. Then, a twenty-two hour period of solid rain culminating in an enormous thunderstorm saw nine inches of rainfall. Only twice, since record-keeping began, has such a volume been exceeded. This ran straight off the land into the streams that empty into the East and West Lyn rivers.

The sheer volume of flood water was not, however, the main cause of the mayhem wreaked on this pretty community. The deluge had washed trees and even animal carcasses into the East Lyn river, and the sheer weight of water was moving large boulders downstream. These were jamming under bridges and damming the water. Eventually, either the bridge or the blockage gave way, releasing a wall of water and debris to surge its way down to the next bridge.

Meanwhile, the West Lyn, which falls 1,500ft in a little over four miles was also in full spate. Bridges over this river had likewise been washed away, the volume of water augmented by the failure of the bank holding Woolhanger Pond, three miles inland. In Lynmouth, this river had been diverted and culverted into the East river, which it joined at right angles (3), but on that fateful night, this was soon blocked. Unable to drain naturally, the water flooded into its original course, slightly to the right and a wall of water hit the village, spreading across the delta and wreaking destruction on everything in its path.

By dawn on Saturday, the water level had dropped considerably and the true extent of the devastation was revealed. Thirty-one people had died, 1,000 were homeless, with almost 100 buildings damaged or de-molished. The army were called in to help clear up the mess. Some of the boulders washed down could not be moved by machinery and had to be blasted into smaller pieces.

Subsequently, the channel of the two rivers has been straightened, allowing any excess floodwater to run off quickly. The area of the confluence, once charming houses and hotels is now a car park; recon-struction being deemed too dangerous in the event of a reapeat storm.

Although not predictable, there had been floods of that magnitude in the valley before, with concomitant damage. In 1769, contemporary reports tell that " . . . the river rose to such a degree as was never known by the memory of any man now living . . ."

Today, there is little evidence of the ferocity or horror of that night, but look at the streams, and with a little imagination . . .

The Walk

Cross the road outside the car park and take the path through the gate, past the covered shelter to the right of Lynton and Lynmouth Cricket Club ground. The pavilion is a delicate building, snuggling under the rocks in the far left corner. The club was founded in 1876, and the ground is a wonderfully attractive place to watch the battle of leather and willow.

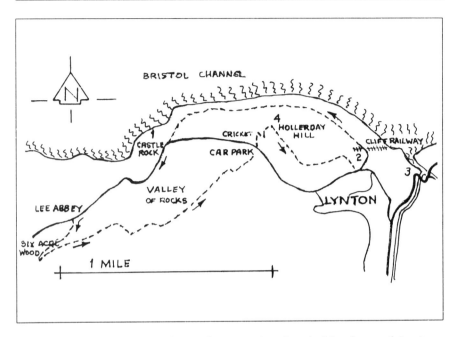

The path climbs steeply through a couple of switchbacks, and is sign-posted to Lynton via Hollerday Hill (4). It is a straightforward if a little crooked walk until it arrives in the town with a mock tudor building to the right. This is the library. On meeting the main road turn left. Walk past the entrance to the cliff railway (2) to North Walk Hill and turn left. This section of the walk is also part of The South West Coastal Path and The Tarka Trail (see Walk 11).

This road crosses the railway and eventually narrows to become a footpath. Before it does so, it passes many hotels and guest houses. One in particular, to the right, is set into the steeply falling cliff in such a way that the road looks down on it. The steep pitched little roofs, turrets, weather vane and gable ends creates a delightful amalgam of angles and corners. This is Hewitts Hotel and Restaurant, the terrace providing a superb view out into the Bristol Channel.

The paved path cut into the hillside now on the seaward side of Hollerday Hill is the result of work by a Mr. Sanford who, in 1817 undertook the task. Successive generations continue to applaud his labours. Follow the path which eventually turns inland, with the bulk of Castle Rock (1) ahead. Pass to the landward side of this and join the road heading west.

Quite often, you will see a herd of goats grazing this area. They are Cheviots, introduced in the 1980s by Lynton Town Council. This is the only wild herd in the south of England and replaces the feral Saanen goats that had been here since the 19th century.

Pass through the gate which gives entry into the Lee Abbey estate, and as you reach the house on the right, look for a gateway and signpost to the left, leaving The Tarka Trail which continues down the road. Cross the field, climbing gently, and into Six Acre Wood.

After 300 yards, there is a track to the left that almost doubles back on itself. Take this and continue the gentle climb out of the woods, over a field and into uncultivated hillside that needs another switchback to climb to the top of the south side of The Valley of Rocks. The path continues along the top of the escarpment for over half a mile before a signposted path leads down off the heights and back into the car park.

Walk 3:
Ilfracombe – Slade Reservoirs – Leebridge

The Victorian town of Ilfracombe was once a typically English seaside resort. Sadly, it has now acquired a reputation for tawdriness which it is still trying to shed. Crime and drugs are a major problem: by Devonian standards. Compared to our larger cities, they probably register about .0001 on the Richter Scale. The DSS "Bed and Breakfast" culture, strong in the town, makes it an uphill battle, but one that must be won before this pretty town can return to its former glory.

Distance: 6 miles

Terrain: Steady uphill climb on outward leg, steady descent on return. One sharp uphill almost at the finish.

Refreshment: Nothing outside the town.

Map: 180

Grid Reference: SS 516467

Starting Point: The Coach House Inn, Bicclescombe Park Road, Ilfracombe. This is a very sharp right turn approaching the town off the A361. A large board advertising Bicclescombe Park has a smaller Coach House sign attached.

Transport: Regular bus service to Barnstaple. National Express coach services from many towns and cities throughout the country.

Another free house, The Coach House Inn is one of the less architecturally interesting buildings covered in this book. It's got "oak beams" that seem *de rigueur* in this type of place, and a very interesting restaurant upstairs specialising in locally caught fish. Bar snacks are also available, and the pub serves food twice a day every day; very handy when trying to get a meal on Sunday evening. The main beers come from Bass, but always with a guest beer on tap. There are "things" everywhere. The landlord describes it as "clutter, rubbish and junk", but the overall effect created is warm and welcoming.

Glazed tiles make up the letters of a street sign in Ilfracombe. (photo: Elizabeth Fowler)

The Barnstaple and Ilfracombe Railway

This was a most spectacular railway; operationally. For those who enjoyed the sight and sound of steam locomotives hard at work, the departure from Ilfracombe took some beating. No sooner had the trains left the station bound for Barnstaple than they were battling up a 1 in 36 gradient – very steep by railway standards. This did not ease until the line approached Mortehoe. It was then a long downhill run to Braunton.

The line was over twenty years in the planning, and work did not start until 1871. Opened to great celebrations on July 21st 1874, it was originally single track, but was doubled towards the end of the 1880s to help cope with the sheer volume of traffic. The railway made Ilfracombe. Prior to its arrival, the only way in was a difficult coach ride, or by ship. Sea trips from south Wales were already popular, but the town really became a resort with the arrival of trains.

Eventually, there were through trains from London Waterloo, and the famed Atlantic Coast Express terminated in the town. The Great Western Railway also got in on the act. They ran summer Saturday specials from London Paddington to Taunton, and via Exmoor and Barnstaple. Pullman luxury in the form of The Devon Belle was available for a few years after the last war, but lack of trade saw it removed. The line began its run-down at the same time as many of our railways, although it survived the initial Beeching axe. Steam trains were withdrawn on September 5th 1964 and the ubiquitous diesel railcar replaced them. Trains were few, and times inconvenient. All through services were discontinued, and the line reduced in status to a branch. The end came on October 20th 1970 when the line, by then a shadow of its former self was finally put out of its misery, just a few years short of a centenary celebration.

Cairn Nature Reserve

This 19 acre site is owned by the council, but leased to The Devon Wildlife Trust. A century ago it was rough hill grazing, but in 1911 was planted with a mix of deciduous and coniferous trees. There are over 200 types of flowering plants on the Cairns, and the somewhat unkempt nature of the reserve make it a wonderful home for wild life. Many types of birds can be seen, with Black Caps and Chiff-chaff overwintering here.

The Walk

Leave the pub, return to the main road and turn right. About 50 yards along is The Dorchester Hotel. To the left is a flight of steps by a letter box and bus stop. Turn up these. At the top is a track. Turn right for a few yards, and then left up the tarred road. Opposite is a factory, Pall Ilfracombe. This is built on the site of the old railway station. Sympatheti-cally constructed to blend with its surroundings, the company have received several awards for its design. With over 250 employees, one of the largest in the town, Pall manufacture sophisticated filtration systems for demanding users in the food and pharmaceutical industries.

At the end of this road is a narrow, almost unmarked track on the left. This is the walk, alongside Cairns Nature Reserve. It climbs up a fair gradient for about 200 yards before easing. This is a good place to pause, turn and look out to sea. If visibility is reasonable, the Welsh coast can be seen across the Bristol Channel. This is the Swansea area. The higher ground is Cefn Bryn, and, at dusk, the lighthouse flashing is at Mumbles Head. Closer, across the valley is the National Trust land at Torrs Park, and Langleigh.

Some 250 yards along this path, take the track off to the right. A flight of steps follow which leads down to the course of the railway. Once upon

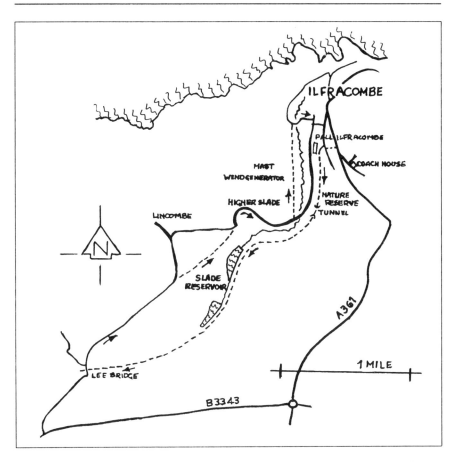

a day, this was alive with trains, particularly on summer weekends. To the right were carriage sidings where holiday excursions waited until departure time. Just over the fence, a turntable was located. Turn left and start the long climb. A easy grade for walkers, this was where steam engines grafted away, smoke and sparks being blasted skyward by the effort. There is an interesting little curio of the railway age to be seen on the left after a few yards. On a tiny bridge, the post here still carries the white stencilled legend "225.65". This is the distance, in miles and chains, to London Waterloo station. A short twin bore tunnel appears, The right-hand one is blocked, but with holes at the top. This is to encourage bats to roost. An old signal arm still exists, with a platform and lamp holder up high.

Slade reservoirs are close to the right as the walk grinds inexorably uphill, but a cutting with bridge overhead presages the summit. A couple of yards beyond the next road bridge is a footpath sign on the right, pointing towards Lee. Turn here and take the narrow country lane heading north east. 1200 yards along here, as the road takes a left, is a new house on the right-hand side. Just beyond, a gate and Footpath sign point right. Through the field heading slightly to the right, and at the next hedge, a stile with waymark arrow affixed points down the slope to a gate. This leads into a pretty green lane. At the end, another gate into a paved lane. Turn right down the hill. High on the left is a radio mast and one of the new windmill generators making a slight but continuous whirring sound; disconcerting for those living too close.

Below are the reservoirs, and on the other side of the valley it is possible to pick out the course that the walk recently followed. In Higher Slade, an unmarked Right of Way leads off to the left just past a new house and before a gate into a field. This narrow track, to the left of the hedge is difficult to follow, but is there for the more adventurous. It lead around a hillside before plunging downhill towards Langleigh.

The easier walk is to follow the road around, past the water treatment works to a signpost on the left marked Public Bridleway, through what appears to be a private gate. The houses here, in Lower Slade are strikingly different depending on which side of the road you live. To the left are stern old stone terraced cottages, lovingly modernised. On the right, modern brick which improve this attractive area not one jot.

Follow the bridleway across three fields to a narrow lane which serves as a drive to houses. Here, if you have followed the difficult path, the walks will reunite. At the end of that lane turn right, down into the dip and then up the steep hill which is Broad Park Avenue. At the "T" Junction turn right into Broad Park Crescent, and first left into Richmond Road. After 100 yards, as the road swings left, take the secondary road to the right; Station Road. Walk up here, and at the top is the junction from the start of the walk. Bear left, turn left down the steps and back to the pub.

Walk 4:
Mortehoe – Morte Point – Bull Point

With its mainly west-facing cliffs, this walk, which includes a short length of the Coastal Footpath is a favourite for early evening during the summer. With the sun sinking gently in the west, the Lundy ferry *M.S. Oldenberg* in passage to Ilfracombe and few tourists about, it can be sheer bliss.

Distance: 4½ miles

Terrain: Generally easy, a couple of short climbs on the Coast Path section.

Refreshment: All varieties in Mortehoe.

Map: 180.

Grid Reference: SS 456454

Starting Point: The Ship Aground, Mortehoe.

Transport: Red Bus (01271 45444) and Filers (01271 863819) operate services (Not Sundays) from Ilfracombe and Red Bus service 654 runs from Barnstaple on Tuesdays and Fridays only.

There is an embarrassment of riches at the start of this walk. Within a couple of hundred yards, the Smugglers Rest, The Chichester Arms and The Ship Aground vie for trade. The latter is the only one offering a local beer and cider: Hancock's Devon Cider, a heady brew, made in South Molton (see Walk 10), and Cottleigh's Tawny Ale, brewed in Wiveliscombe on Exmoor.

Add in Boddington's, Flowers Original, food from 11am to midnight during the summer, and 11am to 2.15pm and 6pm to midnight in winter, served in a delightfully twee setting, and the overall effect is marvellous. And, next door is a fish and chip shop, followed by a café serving Cream Teas: 'nuff said! Not that the opposition lags far behind: try them all and see.

Mortehoe

An attractive village suffering acutely from seasonal holidaymakers. Its proximity to Woolacombe – with which it used to share a train station –

and the Coastal Path ensure its popularity. The name is believed to be derived from *morte* – death, and *hoe* – hill, very appropriate given the cliffs here. A theory advanced a couple of centuries ago attributed the name to a pre-historic burial ground nearby. This was never proved, but remains an interesting possibility.

There are the (almost) standard Devonian village features with low beamed thatched and whitewashed cottages, pubs, and the church of St. Mary Magdalene looking out to sea: and an intriguing – and ongoing – legend attached. A tomb within the South transept is alleged to be that of William de Tracy, one of Thomas à Beckett's murderers.

In his admirable 1630s Survey of Devon, Tristram Risdon states. "In this remote place sir William Tracy, son of Oliver lord Tracy lived a private life . . . Certain it is, [after the murder] he withdrew himself hither to spend the remainder of his life, and lieth buried in an aisle of this church, by him built, under an erected monument, with his portraiture engraven on a grey marble stone . . ."

Regrettably, none of it is true. The William de Tracy referred to was actually vicar of the church and died in 1322. The style of the tomb established beyond doubt that it belonged to that century. Over the years, it has been badly defaced by those who thought they were attacking the murderer's resting place. When opened in the last century, the tomb was empty. Whether it was grave robbers in search of the lead sheet in which he would have been buried, or someone intent on desecration cannot be known. What is certain is that the simple fact of carrying the name "Tracy" ensured that the poor priest would never rest in peace. The errant Sir William's remains are firmly established as lying in Copsenza, a town in the southern tip of Italy. There is some very attractive stained glass in the church, and the whole building is delightfully original, having suffered only lightly at the hands of Victorian "restorers" in 1857.

The Coast

Yet another area that saw the death of many a hardy seafarer. The rocks of Bull Point and Morte Point ripped the bottoms from dozens of sturdy ships. In the winter of 1852, no less than five vessels were lost on Morte. Despite its history of tragedy, the whole area is outstandingly beautiful: the National Trust agree, having taken most of it under their wing. Looking north from Bull Point, the South Wales coast can be picked out on a clear day.

Barricane Beach, a delightful sandy cove south of Morte is famed for the number and variety of sea shells washed up. It can be reached down a steep path and is a very pleasant place to get away from the crowds should you be given to sunbathing.

The rugged South West Coastal Path skirts the of Rackham Bay. (photo: Elizabeth Fowler)

Bull Point

It was as recently as 1879 that a lighthouse was first built here. The 35ft high tower holds a paltry 1500 watt light, but the optics allow its beam to be seen for 25 nautical miles. It is automatic, but there is a keeper on station who opens the tower to visitors providing it does not interfere with his other duties.

This lighthouse is quite new. In September 1972, part of the cliff fell into the sea causing walls in the previous building to crack and partially collapse, and the whole structure to be declared unsafe. A temporary light-ship was provided by Trinity House until a new building was ready, and the existing equipment, new in 1960, installed and working.

The old foghorn that roared like a bull is now (mercifully) silent: deemed redundant in this technological age.

The Walk

Only The Chichester Arms has anything resembling a car park. There is a Pay and Display on the edge of the village almost opposite The Smugglers Rest. From there, turn left and follow the road to The Ship Aground, past The Chichester Arms and down the hill. On the left is Mortehoe Gift Shoppe, and below, on the right a Public Footpath leading over a small rise, down a track, past the cemetery onto open land and the

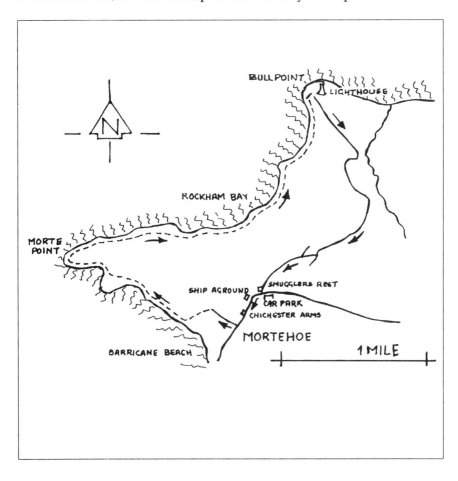

Coastal Path. There are numerous ways across this NT land. Heading towards the left, the walk soon gains the cliff tops and a remarkable view back to Barricane Beach, Woolacombe the vast beaches of Morte Bay and Baggy Point.

On reaching the cliffs, turn right and follow the clearly marked path around Morte Point towards Rockham Bay, a couple of gentle descents followed by a couple of equally gentle ascents before reaching the lighthouse at Bull Point.

From the Point, a metalled road leads inland. There is no deviation from this, giving a clear path back into Mortehoe. On regaining the road proper, follow it down past the Rockham Bay Hotel, much favoured by touring coach parties and back to the Smugglers Rest. Across the road, just a little to the left is the car park.

Walk 5:
West Down – Beara Down –
Lower Aylescott

This is North Devon at it rural best. Plenty of road sections here with hardly a vehicle around, making easy walking. Lush greenery with only livestock and the occasional tractor to disturb the bucolic peace.

Distance: 7 miles.

Terrain: Hilly, but only 2 short steep sections.

Refreshment: Only at the Start/Finish

Map: 180

Grid Reference: SS 516421

Starting Point: The Crown Inn, West Down.

Transport: Virtually none. One 'bus to/from Barnstaple on Tuesdays and Fridays only. Barnstaple to Ilfracombe services operate along the main road half a mile away. Details 01271 382800.

The Crown is a gem. Creeper covered walls, lots of odd-shaped rooms, and Whitbread's Ales. There is a garden, and food is served lunchtimes and evenings. It's popular with the locals, and just far enough from the tourist routes to avoid being over-run by them.

West Down

Now a place much favoured as a commuter village; if such a term can be applied to the handful who live here and work in Barnstaple. It was for centuries a very poor village with an agriculturally-based economy. Almost 200 years ago there were a mere 200 residents, almost half of whom were registered as "Paupers". There are 3 farms recorded in Domesday and the church is early 1300s. One oddity about this building can be seen from the outside. The clock in the tower has a diamond shaped surround holding the blue face and gold hands.

The elegant sign outside The Crown Inn at West Down. (photo: Elizabeth Fowler)

Fullabrook Mine

There are few records of the working of this mine. All that is known for certain is that it produced manganese. The same seam was also worked at Braunton, Combe Martin and Shirwell.

The Walk

Leave the pub and cross the road to the right-hand corner of The Long House tea room. There, take the road to the left leading past the Post office with the churchyard and church to the left. Almost level with that building is a house on the right called Austins Hay which has a gravel drive. This is a Public Footpath and leads shortly to a stile. Straight across two more stiles to a lane; turn right.

After 150 yards, follow a track downhill to the left. This passes Wood Lane Cottage, which has long tailed bats and dormice resident in the roof. As the path reaches a stream on the left, a gate takes the walk straight ahead into fine deciduous woodland and uphill alongside the valley. Reaching this particular summit, the path leaves the wood and heads across a field before starting its plunge into the next valley. The route describes something of a "Z" over the next quarter of a mile, passing through a smallholding where the exit gate is to the low side of the barn. The next stile is halfway down the field on the right-hand side. Over the stile and follow the path along the contour before heading gently downhill through a wooded section towards the river.

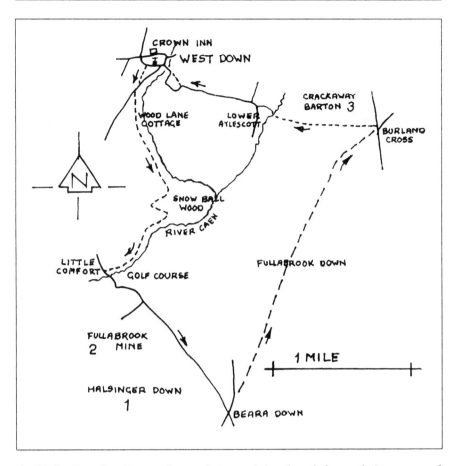

At Little Comfort Farm, the path is straight ahead through 2 gates and into the lane. Turn left, cross the bridge, and walk up the hill which is steep for a short distance before easing. Soon, a pause at the gate on the left gives a glorious view back across the valley, graphically showing "Z" you have just walked.

Continue straight ahead, the skyline on the right being Halsinger Down (1). The viewpoint mentiond in Walk 6 is just over the other side. Nearer, a tree lined valley runs parallel with the road, with a clump of bushy trees at one point. This was Fullabrook Mine (2).

At the end of this lane, on Beara Down, turn left, and after 200 yards, follow a green lane leaving to the right. Over 2 miles long, it is uphill for most of its course, and initially is well-used by farm vehicles. After half a mile, all the tractors turn right into a field, leaving ferns and brambles in charge. This continues until the lane starts to go downhill, when farm usage makes it easily passable again.

There is a gate and stile at the end of this lane. Immediately alongside on the left is another gate, with a green lane to its right. This is the walk. Pass through a gate and follow the hedge to the left down the field. The farm on the hillside is Crackaway Barton (3), first recorded in 1242.

At the far end, the path enters woodland, crosses the infant river Caen which features in Walk 6, and turns immediately right into a narrow track, uphill, round to the left, and passing Lower Aylescott on the left before reaching a lane. Head uphill, straight ahead, and follow this for the next half mile. As the lane descends towards West Down, pleasantly visible at successive farm gates, look out for a Public Footpath sign off to the right. This crosses 2 fields and cuts off the large arc followed by the road. At the exit stile back into the lane, there is a ford on the right giving entrance to a farmer's field. The road is now uphill. Take the first on the right, and follow this round, past the manor house and the church, back to the Crown.

Walk 6:
Braunton – Halsinger – Boode

With magnificent views from Halsinger Down, pleasant strolls through Devon's leafy "Green Lanes" and a very good starting pub, this walk has pretty well everything. But choose a clear day; the views demand it.

Distance: 7 miles.

Terrain: 1 climb to nearly 500ft and down again. Several smaller hills. Quite strenuous

Refreshment: Braunton, the "Largest Village in Devon" has all kinds of refreshments including fish and chips at Squires on the main road. They are regular winners of the South West of England Fish and Chip Shop of the Year award.

Map: 180.

Grid Reference: SS 489371.

Starting Point: The Black Horse, Church Street. Leaving Braunton on the A361 Ilfracombe road, take the right-hand turn (un-named) across from the fire station. Past the church the road swings to the right and the pub is 200 yards along on the left.

Transport: Choice of 'bus services between Barnstaple and Ilfracombe. Details 01271 382800

The Black Horse is still very much a pub; no food, and few of the modern trimmings. But the beer is good with Whitbread Best and Flowers on tap, and Murphy's stout. The building dates from 1646 and still has some of the original beams on show. There is only one bar, but with a mass of activity crammed into it. Skittles, shove ha'penny and darts are all available. This is the pub the locals use.

Braunton

Another village established by a Welsh Saint; Brannoc. There is a lovely legend as to how the beautiful church became established. Brannoc undertook construction on a nearby hill, but each night, the devil undid his labours. Then, in a dream, he was told to seek out a sow suckling her young, there to build his church. This he did the very next day. That site is where St. Brannock's church now stands. The Saint himself is believed buried under the altar, although this majestic building is not the original.

The ruined chapel of St. Michael overlooks st. Brannocks church and graveyard, Braunston. (photo: Elizabeth Fowler)

His chapel was replaced by a collegiate church around 857, which in turn was rebuilt during the thirteenth century. There are some relics from Norman times – particularly the font, and subsequent years have added their own touches. Above the church, atop a hill is St. Michael's chapel (3), a late perpendicular-style ruin built as a votive chapel for seafarers and fishermen. It was a clear landmark from out at sea, and was used as a lookout. Now it is ruined.

The village is still busy today, with a lively centre, very crowded during the holiday season. The traffic, particularly on Saturdays as arriving and departing holidaymakers mix, is frightful. There are several other good pubs closer to the centre of things. Some serve a wonderful array of beers both local and "imported" from the north of England, others seem more interested in taking money from visitors.

The Walk

Leave the pub, walk back to the main road and turn right towards Ilfracombe. 500 yards along, a path departs to the left up a slope. This crosses the old railway (see Walk 3) and follows a path past a very attractive cottage and round a sweeping left-hand bend. Here, turn right, following the Public Footpath sign. This is the first of many "green lanes" on this walk.

Cross a stream, around the base of a hill and alongside the old railway, where a couple of bridges still stand, in fine condition. Then follows quite a sharp climb. Towards the top is a stile on the right. Cross, and head diagonally right over the field, down a very steep slope. The exit stile is in the far right-hand corner. Turn left. This section can be very muddy at times as it follows the river Caen: almost at water level.

Eventually, this path arrives at a road. Turn right, right again and at the main road, left. Cross over, and a path leads off to the right opposite the house. Look at the tall pole in the garden, covered with a creeper. The iron ladder attached shows it is an old railway signal post; we are on the Barnstaple and Ilfracombe Railway again (See walk 3).

The track now is narrow, overgrown and steeply uphill, known locally as Stony Lane. This meets a "proper" road, which the lane (and this walk) cross. The climb has eased considerably, and will soon meet another road coming in from the left.

Turn right here, and a few yards along, almost on the top of Halsinger Down (1), turn right towards Halsinger and Boode. But before you do, pause, looking down that road. This is where you need a clear day. On your right is Lundy, 20 miles out in the Bristol Channel (see Walk 14), to your left is Exmoor, and the hills directly ahead are on Dartmoor: stunning! The wooden poles carrying electricity to surrounding farms are often perches for kestrel or buzzard.

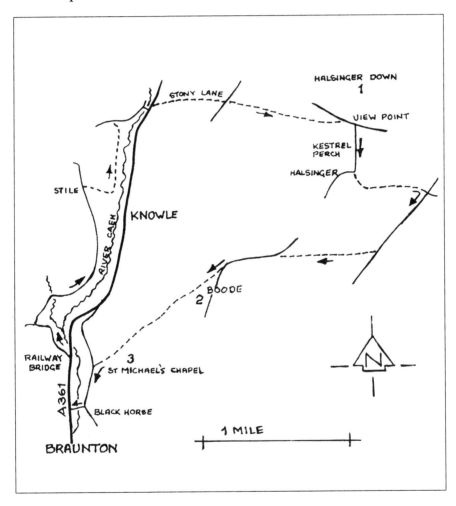

This lane descends for a around a quarter of a mile into the hamlet of Halsinger. Where the road turns right, take the track that goes straight on keeping to the left of the house. This climbs for a short time, turns sharp left and arrives on a paved road. Turn right, and follow this for over half mile until an unmarked but clearly defined green lane bears off to the right. This leads to another metalled road where the walk bears left. Fortunately, as is the norm in this area, virtually the only traffic you will see is from farms: tractors, combine harvesters, and mums on the school run. No public transport up here, and too hilly to cycle for most youngsters, making the family car essential.

The settlement of Boode is next (2), all built around the farm. The old cottages are no longer vital to the retention of farm labour as machinery has virtually taken over. They have been tastefully renovated and are used as summer holiday lets. As the road bears left, take the track that runs straight on, the large sheep shed to your left. This green lane eventually plunges steeply downhill with a rocky surface needing care. On the hill to the left is St. Michael's Chapel (3). This path leads into the village lane. Bear left opposite the church, and back to the pub.

Walk 7:
Pilton – Ashford – West Ashford – Pottington

There is not much urban walking in north Devon, Barnstaple being the only town of any size, but this walk includes some. In medieval times, the major community was Pilton. This was because the hills along the Taw estuary made it defensible. Barnstaple was only a settlement at the lowest fordable point on the river. For the etymologically inclined, the crossing point was marked by a post: *stapol* placed by a chap called *Bearda*. This walk takes in a little of Pilton after some lovely countryside.

Distance: 6 miles

Terrain: Quite easy – by Devonian standards. Only a couple of gentle uphill sections.

Refreshment: Nothing until the last mile, then a full range of pubs, fast foods and a café.

Map: 180

Grid Reference: SS 551342

Starting Point: The Windsor Arms, Bradiford, Barnstaple.

Transport: Barnstaple's Bus Station is about 1 mile away.

The Windsor Arms is one of the rarer free houses in north Devon: completely impervious to the tourist trade. The Tap Room is traditional in the fullest sense of the word with a long trestle table in bare wood and forms for seats. But it's comfortable and busy. It does let itself down badly though in one respect: Sky Television. On soccer nights, it becomes the centre of attraction: sad. The Lounge is smart and the owner friendly. Beers are by Whitbread, the cask ale is Bass, and there is Strongbow Cider on draught.

Ashford

A tiny hillside village, the centre of which is unaffected by the holiday-making area around; caravan sites and everything associated with them. The views over the Taw estuary are quite superb with expanses of sand flats at low tide.

The church of St. Peter is the only building of note in the village. This was completely rebuilt in Victorian times, much of it appearing to be a copy in miniature of Saints Peter and Paul in Barnstaple. As befits its ancestry, much of the interior is plain, although there is a remarkable fourteenth century sculpture of St. John to be found in the vestry.

Pilton

A place of real antiquity. Once the major settlement in the area, Barnstaple had overtaken it by Domesday, with Pilton now very much a suburb. On the hill here around 880, King Alfred built a *burh*, one of only four in Devon. These were fortified places for defence against marauding Danes. In 893, it was a vital part of the English defences as about 40 ships besieged the place, a further 100 attacking Exeter to the south. Alfred rushed reinforcements westwards, but the Danes retreated before battle could be joined. Pilton had done its job.

Almshouses in Pilton. (photo: Alison Fowler)

Pilton Priory And Church

The Priory disappeared in 1536, one of the earliest establishments to suffer from the growth of non-conformism. By then, it was already in terminal decline, having only three occupants. It was a cell of Malmesbury Abbey, founded during the 12th century. The site was to the north of St Mary the Virgin. This was originally the priory church, built around 1320 and has some very handsome work inside. There are two screens of great antiquity, and the tester over the font is unusual and ornate. The main street is a charming hotchpotch of styles and vintages; the sort of place that is full of character and will probably never happen again. It's a sobering thought that much of the aesthetic attraction of these places existed before town planners exercised their malign influence over proposals to construct anything the slightest bit out of the ordinary.

The Walk

Leave the pub and turn right down the hill. Follow the lane for just over half a mile, past Lions Mill and the first Public Footpath sign, to the crest of a hill. Here on the left is another sign pointing towards a stile to the right of a white house – Sunnyview. Into the field, head towards the left, through a gate in the far right corner, and pass a copse on your left before heading towards a gate to the right of some farm buildings. Through this gate, turn left, and after a few yards, the lane drops down into the farmyard. Here, keep right. There is a telephone pole just to the right, and beyond, four trees. Stand by the pole and aim for the second tree on the right. Walk in a straight line past the tree, and the next stile is beyond. Through there, follow the track along the contour and through a gate into an unmade road and into Ashford.

Turn right at the end, and then right again, up the hill and fork left at the church. Turn left by The Old Rectory. A Public Footpath sign points the way, alongside signs to Glebe House and By Ways. This narrow fenced path winds between the houses onto a lane. Turn left and at the end the path is to the right-hand side of a garage. 20 yards down, a stile to the right leads across the top of two gardens to another stile.

Cross this one, and walk through a gateway, past the linhay (cowshed) and immediately turn right at a Waymarked gate. Within a few yards, another Waymarked gate takes the walk to the left. Straight ahead now, over two stiles close together, through two fields, to the lane and turn left. The Taw esuary is laid out below in all its splendour.

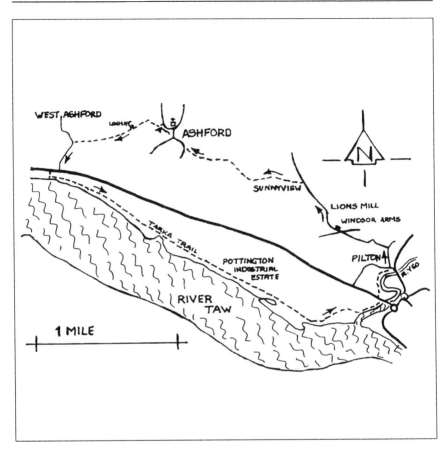

Just before this lane, according to the map, a Right of Way descends to the main road, but as there is no exit from the field at the bottom, your choice of route should be into the lane. On reaching the busy main road turn right and cross. After a few yards, a track leads to the estuary, and immediately across a bridge over the old railway line, now The Tarka Trail (see Walk 11) and The South West Coastal Path. A stile on the right gives access to the track bed, turn right, under the bridge. This offers a very pleasant easy walk back towards Barnstaple, but beware. It is a cycle track and whilst most are thoughtful and enjoying the scenery as much as you are, the occasional head-down-90mph merchant will approach you almost noiselessly giving quite a fright as he whizzes past.

Past the rear of Pottington Industrial Estate – not as unpleasant as it may sound – and the posts of Barnstaple Rugby Club reach for the sky.

Here, beyond a gate, the track bears left, and is well-signposted into Mill Road. Along this road, a sign directs you right up an un-named short narrow street, over a ramp to the river Yeo. Turn left, along Rolle Quay. This was once a railway siding, but extensive work in 1987 turned it into an attractive area with parking spaces. Across the river is home for the sand barges mentioned in Walk 16.

At the end of the quay, turn left by the Rolle Quay Hotel (Free House), cross the road, and 50 yards along on the right is a Cycleway which leads to a high embankment alongside the river. This sweeps in a semi-circle before reaching a wall. A sharp left here brings you to a road.

Turn right and then immediately left past The Reform Inn (Free House) into Pilton Street. Pass The Chichester Arms (Courage) and to the top of the street turning left past the almshouses, down Under Minnow Road, up the hill and along to the Windsor Arms.

This last section was chosen advisedly. It is possible to avoid the centre of Pilton by turning left here and after 150 yards turning right along a Public Footpath, by the school, regaining the walk about 200 yards from the finish. This misses a road section, but also misses the delights of Pilton.

Walk 8:
Marwood – Westcott Barton –
Pippacott – Prixford

A walk of considerable contrasts, mainly through lush valleys, but with the inevitable sea view never too far away. There are several streams around; this walk covers four. They all combine to form Knowl Water, which, in quick succession empties into the river Caen, the Taw, and the Bristol Channel.

Distance: 5½ miles

Terrain: Mainly good underfoot, with several not too steep hills.

Refreshment: Up to 3 places offering "Cream Teas". Exact number depends on the time of year

Map: 180

Grid Reference: SS 549368

Starting Point: The Ring 'o Bells, Prixford. The village is on an unclassified road about 3 miles north west of Barnstaple. The pub is along a side road to the east of the village.

Transport: There is no public transport any nearer than Barnstaple.

The Ring 'o Bells is an extensive free house that appears somewhat schizoid. It tries very hard to retain the "olde worlde country pub" image, but doesn't entirely succeed, although it should. Some of the original buildings are believed to date back to the 16th century. There is a skittle alley and plenty of other pub games including Shove Ha'penny. This is counterpointed by some rather glitzy fittings and a good menu that show an earnest desire to attract the tourist. For all that, there is a good atmosphere other than summer weekends, and the mainly Whitbread beers seem to be of good quality. Star ale though, is undoubtedly Flowers Original.

Marwood Hill Gardens

The owner, Jimmy Smart, started work on his famed garden soon after the last war. A doctor at Sticklepath (Barnstaple), he moved to Marwood, first to The Old Rectory before moving to his present home. An acknowledged world expert on camellias, the gardens are a riot of colour throughout the year, but in spring when the camellia bloom, the sight is shatteringly beautiful. Allow at least 2 hours to appreciate them fully.

The beautiful Marwood HillGardens. (photo: Elizabeth Fowler)

Westcott Barton

This was once the family home of the Chichesters, an ancient family who arrived in Devon from Sussex in the late fourteenth century to marry into the Raleigh family of Barnstaple. One of the descendants of this long line was Sir Francis, the first round-the-world yachtsman. The building is part medieval, but was extensively rebuilt in the 1600s. It is a first class example of a Devonian Barton; the part of an estate that the lord of the manor kept in his own hand. There is also evidence of an old mill. Ann and Robin Gray have succumbed to the visitor trade; but in a rather special way. Robin is a potter, and examples of his fine craftsmanship are on sale. It is also possible to see where he works and how his rather startling designs come into being. The retail area is open from the beginning of April to the end of September. Ann is the caterer. Bed and breakfast is available throughout the year, and cream teas when the pottery is open.

St Michael and All Saints – Marwood

This is one of the more interesting churches featured between these covers. Not only does it stand on a magnificent site with views over a wooded valley, but the fittings inside are many and varied: and unusual. A sundial was supplied by John Berry in 1762. There are many of his sundials still to be found in Devon, but Marwood's shows not only the local time, but also in the principal capitals of Europe and in Jerusalem. The gentleman did exceed this once. The sundial at St. Peter, Tawstock, just to the south of Barnstaple also has details of the time in Cairo, Babylon and Port Royal!

The font cover is of great local interest. It is an early sculpture by John Robinson and shows Simeon blessing the young Jesus at His presentation in the Temple. John was originally a farmer in Australia, but moved to this country in the early 1970s to try and establish his reputation as a sculptor. He moved into The Old Rectory after Jimmy Smart and used the large barn alongside as his studio. His talent soon showed through and commissions started arriving from around the world, including one from Brisbane (Australia). His smaller figures were worked in red wax with clay for the larger ones, and taken to London for casting in bronze. A need to be closer to the major London galleries saw him leave the area after about five years, but his legacy includes two works in the gardens.

The Walk

Leave the pub and follow the lane back to the "main" road. Turn right and follow this road for about half a mile to Guineaford. Care is needed along here as the road carries more traffic than we are used to on Devon lanes. Marwood Methodist Church is on the right, grey and unprepossessing from outside, but inside with a little more interest than is usual in buildings of this type. At the staggered crossroads, the left turn is signed Marwood Hill. Along this lane is the Church Room which serves afternoon teas on Sundays and Bank Holidays from Easter to the end of September between 2.30pm and 5.30pm, and to larger parties by arrangement. Beyond is the splendour of Jimmy Smart's garden after which the road bends to the left and arrives outside the church. Keep to the right of this building, down the hill to the bottom.

Here, leave the road and go straight ahead to the right of a house. This track swings sharp right and then left before arriving at a gate. Pass through and keep the hedge beyond close to your right shoulder. Up a gentle rise to the far end where a Waymark sign points to the right over a stile. Follow this to the end of the tree line, and, just before a fence surrounding a house, turn left. A tree carries the yellow arrow indicating a stile in the bottom right-hand corner. Cross it and turn right into a narrow lane.

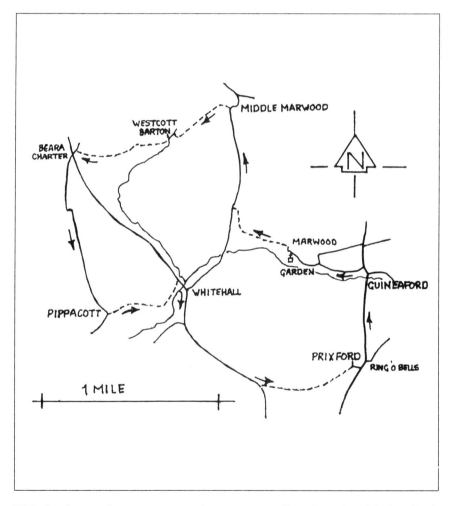

This leads gently up a most picturesque valley. Lovely old thatched cottages, one with a small pond infested by mallards, and Tathill Wood to the right. Almost unnoticed, the occasional house becomes a hamlet. This is Middle Marwood – although there is nothing to tell you. As the road turns sharp right, a path to the left by Alderhurst Cottage leads uphill for a few yards and as it flattens out, on the right a steep flight of wooden steps – a staircase without the hand rail – lead to a stile. Across the field, and the exit is through a gate a shade to the left of straight across. This in turn leads to a Waymarked gate on the right into a farm yard. Follow the path left, right and left again to a metalled road. Turn left.

The buildings ahead are Westcott Barton. Follow the road into the courtyard, and the footpath exit is at the far right-hand side to the left of the house. Do not let the green lawn and garden fool you; this is the Right of Way. Cross the stream on a delicate little bridge and turn left. Pass through the next gate, and immediately on the right is a small wicket gate leading into a steep field. The exit gate is in the upper left-hand corner, which, until you are almost there, looks like an impenetrable thicket.

Through this next field, keeping the hedgerow to your right shoulder and at the far end is a gate into a road. Take the lane straight across signed "Pippacott". This is narrow and banked on both sides. There is a gate towards the end on the right that allows a breathtaking view over fields to the distant Bideford Bay. In Pippacott, the road takes a sharp right. On the left, slightly concealed around the corner, is a gate with Waymark arrow leading to another stile and an almost tunnel-like green lane. Each side is slightly banked, and trees overhang to create the most striking effect.

Another stile leads into Woodland Trust territory with its attendant broadleaf trees, with a delightfully unkempt appearance. Shortly the track forks: take the right-hand (downhill) one. At the next gate, turn right and follow this lane for about 1,000 yards, past 2 junctions, to a track on the left. There is a Public Footpath sign, but it is overgrown. Reaching the next farm, take the track that bears right to the road at the top. Turn left, and the lane to the pub is a few yards along on the right.

```
┌─────────────────────────────────────────────────┐
│  ┌───────────────────────────────────────────┐   │
│  │              Walk 9:                       │   │
│  │  Clifton – Arlington – Churchill           │   │
│  └───────────────────────────────────────────┘   │
└─────────────────────────────────────────────────┘
```

If this walk appears to have more instruction than normal, appearances do not deceive. There many more turns and semi-concealed entrances than usual. For all that, it's great fun and in rapid succession is magnificent/intimate/pretty/stark.

Distance: 6 miles (6½ with diversion – see text)

Terrain: Hilly

Refreshment: Nothing outside start/finish

Map: 180

Grid Reference: SS 600415

Starting Point: The Pyne Arms, Clifton, half a mile west of A39 Barnstaple to Lynton road.

Transport: One 'bus each way on Tuesdays and Friday to Brockham Bridge: Red Bus service 13 – Details from 01271 45444.

The pub is another Devon special. Long low buildings joined together, parts of it over 400 years old, with the road immediately outside the end windows. It sits on a sharp bend with one part almost at right angles to the other. Inside it's a crazy jumble of rooms, all seemingly on different levels; a load of character.

It's a free house, with a frankly uninspiring selection of beer: Courage Directors and John Smith's are the 2 main ones. Fine, if that's your taste. The food can be good, served every day. Opening hours are from 11.30am to 2.30pm and 6pm to 11pm.

Arlington Court

This was another of the Chichester homes. At their height, there were over a dozen branches of this famous Devonian family. That they should have become widespread is not surprising given that Amias, who died in 1577 sired no less than nineteen sons; and four daughters for good measure. This singular fact is referred to in Charles Kingsley's novel Westward Ho! Now, in common with so many, their numbers are few, their circumstances somewhat reduced.

The Pyne Arms at Clifton. A quaint jumble of rooms and internal angles. (photo: Alison Fowler)

The present Arlington Court was built in 1822 by Thomas Lee, and is one of the less interesting buildings architecturally associated with the Chichester's. They acquired the manor in the fourteenth century. The 2780 acres of building and grounds are now National Trust, bequeathed by Miss Rosalie Chichester. The house is open during the summer, the grounds all year round. Although the building itself has nothing much to commend it, the interior is lavish with sweeping staircases, Tuscan angle-pilasters, and an exquisitely painted ornamental ceiling in the music room. The contents are also of great interest. There is a lovely collection of pewter, model ships and shells.

Outside, the stables house a large assortment of horse-drawn vehicles, with carriage rides available during the season. Shetland ponies and Jacob sheep graze the park, the estate's church is at the east side. Again, there is a distinct lack of ostentation in this building, although the organ, by Vowles of Bristol in 1890 is interesting, the more so because a gas light complete with mantle provides illumination for the organist. There is the most magnificent yew tree to the south of the building, whilst inside, inevitably, most of the memorials are to various members of the Chichester family. The shell was rebuilt by R.D. Gould in 1846, with the tower completed in 1899.

The Walk

Leave the pub and turn right. 300 yards up the hill on the right is School Farm. There is a stile and Footpath sign well-concealed around the corner. The settlement of East Down with its imposing Manor House prominent to the left is on the hillside. Cross the stile. Aim for the gate in the middle of the field, then another one into the next field, keeping close to the hedge. At the bottom of the field is a typical Devon linhay (cowshed). Pass this to the right and in the far corner behind is another gate into a short length of green lane.

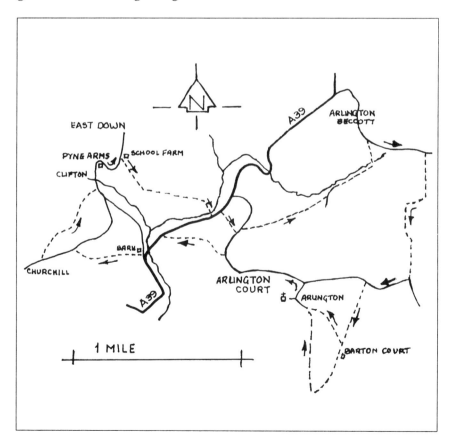

Beyond is an area which, depending on the time of year, is a carpet of bluebells or full of wild raspberries. Down the slope, through a gate and alongside a bank which was once wooded but is now scrub and gorse, for about 250 yards to a stile on the right. This leads across a field, over a narrow bridge crossing the river Yeo to Arlington Mill Farmhouse and up to the main road. Turn left.

This is narrow and busy with no footpath, so care is needed. Fortunately, it is only used for a few yards before a Footpath sign points the way to the right through a coppice just before a pretty thatched cottage. Over a stile, walk up the slope keeping to the fence on the right and out of the gate at the end of that field into a road and turn left. Across, is another gate, unmarked, but a Right of Way. Head half left across the field up the hill aiming for break in the fence. Diagonally left in the next field, though a gateway and continue that course, which leads to two stiles and a green lane. Turn left.

Down this lane, and through a gate is a stream. Keep to the right-hand side of this, crossing a tributary that arrives from the right and to the edge of a wood where a stile awaits. This leads gently uphill through the most enchanting length of woodland with a wide range of British broad-leaf trees and a sheer and ever increasing drop to the chuckling stream on the left. Beech predominates, and with bluebell, periwinkle and rhododendron, the whole area is a delight.

Which is wonderful for the most striking house, standing completely alone at the far end. An idyllic place to live marred only by its situation on a north facing slope which deprives it of sunshine in winter. Beyond, a gate leads the path down to the stream, past a tiny but natural waterfall, over and up the far bank keeping generally right. At the top of the field a gate leads into a green lane which almost immediately arrives at a paved road. Turn right.

Some 350 yards along, a Footpath sign on the right indicates the walk down another green lane. This leads into a field with two gates at the far side. Aim for the right-hand one, pass through it keeping to the left fence until a gate on the left gives access to the next field. Pass through the gate, now keeping close to the right-hand side of this field and at the far end is a gate into a green lane. At the next stile turn right into a metalled road. Continue down the slope for 400 yards out of the woodlands and follow the Footpath sign to the left.

Keeping to the left, pass a gate and to the next stile, which is rather unusual. It's an iron ladder set between two pretty cast iron gateposts. After the next stile, a track leads to the right. This will lead to Arlington.

A half mile diversion is possible here. Continue straight ahead, past Barton Court, an elegant but slightly run-down old farmhouse with several ruined outbuildings. The path swings to the right, and a gate on the left takes the walk down to Deerpark Wood before returning up the slope via a bridleway. Approaching a barn, keep to the left, and a gate leads to a road where the walks re-join.

Ahead, an impressive large stone building is part of the Arlington estate. Pass this to the right. Soon after, a gate on the left gives access to Arlington church, whilst the path continues to another road.

Turn left, past the estate houses and the main entrance to the Court. Further along the lane, a gateway on the left guarded by the Chichester heraldic herons is marked Office and Delivery Entrance Only. Through this gate and turn right, the footpath is along a drive lined with monkey puzzle trees. Pass through a gateway, and 30 yards on the right is the Right of Way. Of this there is no sign. Make your way through the trees to the boundary wall where a break in the stone has a wooden infill, and a stile. Ahead, down the field you can see a wooden barrier in the distance to the right. To the left is a stone barn with red tiled roof. Aim for a point directly between these two where a stile lies hidden. This leads back down to the main road.

Turn left, cross the main road and after 100 yards is a right turn bringing the walk to the previously mentioned barn. Immediately on the left of this barn is a Public Footpath sign which leads steeply uphill. Follow this over a stile and along the rutted track to the road at the end. Turn left towards Churchill. Just beyond the first houses, a fingerpost on the right points the way into a field. The exit stile is in the far left corner. Keep close to the left-hand side of this field, through the gate at the bottom, bearing right down the hill. At the bottom is a road. Turn left, and the pub is a few yards along.

Walk 10:
Alswear – Mariansleigh – Radley

This is the furthest east we get – albeit still well within the administration district known as North Devon. There is nothing of historic or architectural interest, but rolling countryside is of the finest. After 1½ miles, a variety of paths gives the opportunity to "customise" the walk.

Distance: Route "A" – 3½ miles. Route "B" – 5½ miles. Route "C" – 6 miles.

Terrain: Quite hilly.

Refreshment: None apart from the start/finish.

Map: 180.

Grid Reference: SS 725220.

Starting Point: The Butchers Arms, Alswear. On the B3137 Tiverton to South Molton road.

Transport: None, the nearest is a bus service in South Molton, 3 miles to the north.

The Butchers Arms is a fine free house, split into two rooms, one of which is essentially a dining area. The Bar is down to earth, with very few frills, but a warm and welcoming feel to it. It was once on the busy A377 which was the main route into north Devon from "up country", creating a good passing trade. With the opening of the North Devon Link Road (A361) in the mid 1980s, virtually all this traffic has gone.

Some of its trade is seasonal but, throughout the year, if you want Sunday lunch, it is necessary to reserve a table, so great is the demand locally. Courage Directors, Bass, Guinness and Gaymers Cider are available on tap, with John Smiths and Websters staking a claim for northern brews.

Hancocks Devon Cider

A couple of miles to the east is the hamlet of Clapworthy. There, in the old mill, the Hancock family make their cider. For 5 generations now, they have worked in the area, although their presence at this location is new(ish). The site was once a flour mill, and saw subsequent use as a cosmetics factory. Now only the perfume of apples is on offer. Locally

Cider apples and barrels outside Hancocks Cider Works, Clapworthy. (photo: Elizabeth Fowler)

grown cider apples as well, including some from their own orchard behind the works. The annual output is dependent on the harvest, but can be up to 20,000 gallons.

It is possible to visit the works, see the equipment, and watch a film of the actual manufacturing process. There is a picnic area, aviary, and a licenced gift shop giving you the opportunity to take home a bottle of Devonian sunshine. The place is open 9.30am to 1pm, and 2pm to 5pm.

The Walk

Leave the car park, which is on a junction, and turn hard left following the road to Kings Nympton. After a few yards, there is a left turn – still on the Kings Nympton road – and across a pretty bridge. As the road starts uphill, an apparently private drive to New Mill on the left is the footpath, which at the next gate turns to the right over a stile. This path is lined with rose bushes, and presents the most glorious display during summer. The large formal garden belonging to the house is laid out below. A small conifer wood is next, with a fork in the path: take the left down to a gate into a road. Turn left.

After a few yards, at another road junction, turn right, and a stony track on the left after 50 yards is the route of the walk. This leads inexorably uphill, Past Tidlake Farm and eventually through a gate into a field. At the far end of this are two gates. The right-hand one leads into a lane, and a right turn continues the uphill climb.

The entrance to Pitt Farm is a place to pause awhile, get your breath back, and drink in the grandeur of the panorama on your left. A patch-work of fields, each in their different hues fills the foreground, whilst the imposing bulk of Exmoor dominates the skyline: truly magnificent. Eventually, having reached some 600ft above sea level, there is a Public Footpath sign to the left; and the first parting of the ways.

Route "A"

Turn here and follow the path steeply downhill keeping the wooded area to your left. Cross the stream and the path leads into a farmyard. Turn left by the barn, and follow the track, taking a right turn after about 300 yards. At the next farm, turn left and rejoin the other 2 routes (Marked * at the very end of this walk).

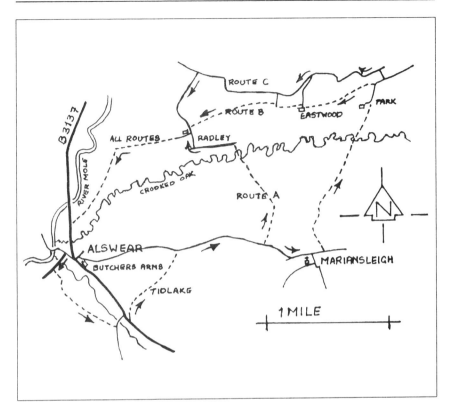

Routes "B" & "C"

The road duly arrives in Mariansleigh, a nondescript hamlet with only limited interest. The church of St. Mary was a 15th century building destroyed by fire in 1932 and subsequently rebuilt. It has a somewhat forbidding exterior, but is surprisingly light and airy inside. The hall opposite is minuscule and houses a letterbox on its walls imprinted "V R". Take the road through the housing signposted "Rose Ash" and some 200 yards along is a green lane to the left.

This rocky path descends into the valley of the Crooked Oak (Yes, that really is the name of the river), into a field, and out at the far side over a narrow bridge and stile. Aim for the gate on the right of the farm which leads into a paddock and then into a lane from the farm. Follow this to the top where it takes a right turn for Route "C".

(ROUTE "B" ONLY) At this point turn left into the field and through the next gate, keeping the thicket to your right. From here, there is no clear track, no Waymarkers and no signposting. A gate leads into the driveway of Eastwood, a "horsey" establishment. Right and immediately left is another gate. Through here, keeping the fence close to your left, and at the far end is a stile. This is singularly difficult to traverse at the moment as a large tree just beyond has blown over, taking much of the banking with it. Only the bole is left now, but to compound the problem, a stream runs in a deepish gully alongside.

When you successfully negotiate this obstacle, a stile at the far side brings you into the yard of Westwood Farm. The exit is to the right and then left across a field, through a gate and beyond to another farm with an elegant house. The lane from the right brings in Route "C", and from the left, Route "A". Take a left turn and then a path to the right between Pear Tree Cottage and a barn leads into a track.

Route "C"

A further 100 yards along this track turns left to a minor road. Then another left, down the hill, over the stream and up the other side with a much gentler gradient, for about 1 mile. As the road starts another downhill section take the left turn to Radley. On reaching the farm buildings, turn right at Pear Tree Cottage as all three routes come together again.

* Follow this lane into and across a field at the end, heading slightly right downhill. A gate in the distance leads into a road where a left turn will bring you back to the Butchers Arms, some 400 yards along.

```
┌─────────────────────────────────────────────────────┐
│ ┌─────────────────────────────────────────────────┐ │
│ │                  Walk 11:                        │ │
│ │     Bishops Tawton – Codden Hill –               │ │
│ │          Bableigh – Landkey                      │ │
│ └─────────────────────────────────────────────────┘ │
└─────────────────────────────────────────────────────┘
```

Walk 11: Bishops Tawton – Codden Hill – Bableigh – Landkey

Forced into a corner and told to choose only one walk, this would probably be it. But only on a clear day. The views from Codden Hill demand it.

Distance: 5½ miles

Terrain: 1 long uphill climb, otherwise easy.

Refreshment: Pub in Landkey.

Map: 180

Grid Reference: SS567301

Starting Point: The Chichester Arms, or The Three Feathers, Narrow Lane, Bishops Tawton. Off the A377 Barnstaple to Crediton road.

Transport: Hourly 'bus service from Barnstaple (not Sundays) details from Red Bus – 01271 45444.

Here again, you will have to make up your own mind what you want from a pub. The Chichester Arms is a gorgeous-looking 16th century thatched building. They serve a vast range of food which all looks very good, and have four real ales. So what's wrong? Nothing you can put your finger on. It's a bit plastic, a bit twee, but if you want food and a choice of four real ales then this is the one for you.

However, if your taste is for the sawdust-and-spittoon (figuratively speaking) pub, The Three Feathers is a winner. Part of the Discovery Inns chain, it exudes character. The pub was opened in 1623 in the building that was already on site. Food is limited to bar snacks, and the real ale is Wadsworth 6X. The landlord says that he works flexi-hours: if someone wants serving he'll serve them, and he is out of the Pub Landlord mould that was broken twenty years ago. The atmosphere is superb, the beer is good and the company convivial. A no-frills pub. Magnificent!

Codden Hill Memorial (1)

This was dedicated on December 4th 1971 by the Archbishop of Canterbury and the Bishop of Crediton as a memorial to Caroline Thorpe, wife of the Rt. Hon. Jeremy Thorpe. He was the former leader of the Liberal Party, and MP for the North Devon constituency at the time. Caroline died in a road accident on June 29th 1970 aged 32. They lived quite close to this spot in Cobbatton. The walk-around cobbled circular base has edging on which is carved compass points, and a note of what can be seen from each one.

Also located at the foot of the monument is a seat, dedicated to Flying Officer Stanley J. H. Verney RAFVR, 1918 – 1943.

Impressive thatch on the Chichester Arms, Bishops Tawton, one of two pubs recommended on this walk. (photo: Elizabeth Fowler)

The Tarka Trail (2)

This is a 180 mile footpath created in the 1980s by Devon Council. It is based (loosely) on the journeys of Tarka the Otter, as told in Henry Williamson's famous book. There is a diverse mixture of walking, from the northern slopes of Dartmoor, through lush lowland, along old railways, and up over Exmoor before following the South West Coastal Path around the northern limits of Devon.

The Walk

Turn left outside The Chichester Arms (or right from The Three Pigeons), and join the main road in the direction of Exeter. After 150 yards take the lane to the left. Immediately, there is a left turn (ignore) and a half-left which is an uphill track. Follow this for a few yards until you reach a gate and then double back left towards a large wooden shed. Here, turn right and start the real ascent of Codden Hill.

Two thirds of the way up the hill is a real parting of the ways with no less than four choices: take the right-hand one. As the climb eases and the path swings around to the right heading more easterly, note the huge quarry across the valley. That looms large (literally) in the walk later. Directly above the quarry face are a couple of houses, and a farm complex. From this range, they look perilously close to the edge.

The views are now starting to register. There really is the most mag-

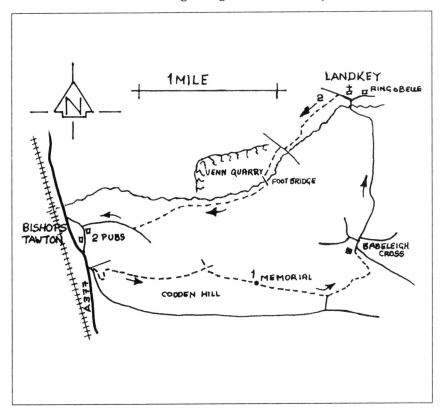

nificent range. At the top, by the memorial (1) the walk has reached 629ft above sea level. For many years, a local tradition saw the villagers from Landkey climbing the hill on the first Sunday in March each year to set fire to the dead bracken. This improved the grazing for their livestock, but must have been a somewhat hazardous venture.

Continue along the track as it starts to descend, gently at first, passing through 2 gates. At the second, take the steep turn to the left into a narrow green lane with the most amazing miscellany of flora on display. What you see depends on the season, but it does sport a wondrous diversity of fungus in the autumn.

After many twists and turns, the path descends into a valley and reaches a paved surface with a bungalow directly ahead, bear right to Bableigh Cross. Here, walk straight across, and continue to walk straight ahead, ignoring the next turn on the right. This lane eventually leads over the river and into Landkey. At the junction, below St. Paul's church, turn left, up the hill for some 150 yards. If you need refreshment, the Ring o' Bells free house is a few yards to the right of the church.

At the top of the rise, a Public Footpath sign points the way to the left. Also attached to the top the gate post is a waymark with a pawprint. This signifies the course of The Tarka Trail (2). Shortly, a gate bars the way, but a narrow path just to the right continues the walk. Over the next stile, take the left fork which leads into a swampy area and on, alongside the river, to a road. Directly across is the quarry that was seen from the top of Codden.

Amazingly the Public Footpath goes right through the works. Cross into the works – keeping a careful lookout for lorries or dump trucks – and follow the road, keeping to the left of the building marked "Workshop", to a barrier. This advises that blasting takes place between 9am and 5pm, and that the footpath is to the left. Cross the river over a small bridge, turn right at the far end and follow the course of the river, around the hillside to the next hedge. The exit stile is about 40 yards up from the river. Over the stile, an electricity pole can be seen. Using this for your bearing, head straight for it, and in the far distance is the exit to the field.

At that gate, head diagonally left, up the hill to another stile. This leads into Sentry Lane. Turn right, walk down the hill back into Bishops Tawton and turn left to reach the pubs.

Walk 12: Eggesford Forest

A waymarked route partly through Forestry Commission lands, using some of The Tarka Trail (see Walk 11) towards the end.

Distance: 8 miles.

Terrain: Generally undulating.

Refreshment: Eggesford Garden Centre have a tea-room.

Map: Almost all on 191, a few yards on 180.

Grid Reference: SS 681119.

Starting Point: The Fox and Hounds at Eggesford on the A377 Crediton to Barnstaple road.

Transport: Eggesford train station on the Tarka Line – Barnstaple to Exeter service.

The Eggesford House Hotel which contains The Fox and Hounds pub is mostly new. Some of the old building can be seen to the right end of the main block. With accommodation for salmon fishermen, its own private section of river, timeshare apartments and private golf course, it may seem a little prepossessing for the *hoi polloi*, but do not let appearances influence you. The bar is a thoroughly friendly place and with draught Wadsworth 6X, Bass and Worthington on offer, the serious drinker will find his needs well catered for. Fancy some fishing? A permit for salmon on their 7 miles of Taw and Little Dart rivers will set you back £18.50 a day or £100.00 a week. A trout permit is a mere £10.00!

Eggesford House

The original building dates back to the mid 13th century in the reign of Henry III. It was sited next to where the church still stands. The owners were the Reigney family who lived there for over 200 years until the last child, a daughter, married a Copplestone. Their only child was also a daughter who married into the Chichester family.

The estate passed through several hands, and the house was rebuilt over the centuries, the last time between 1718 and 1723 by William Fellowes. His nephew, who became the Earl of Portsmouth demolished the house in 1832, rebuilding on a different site: further up the valley, to the north of the original. This magnificent building, variously dated between 1820 and 1830 was home to the Portsmouth's until 1911. During that time, one of the daughters married Augustus Christie, owner of Tapeley Park, Instow whose son John, was the founder of Glyndebourne Opera House in Sussex. The disappearance of Eggesford House was a tragedy. It was offered for sale in 1913 but found no takers. Some of the associated buildings – the Fox and Hounds for instance – were sold, but the main house just crumbled away after having all its interior fittings removed and sold.

Trying to imagine what todays estate agent would have made of the particulars is mind-blowing. There were 6 Reception Rooms, 30 Bedrooms, Domestic Offices, Servants Quarters, stabling for 40 horses, but only 2 Bathrooms; clearly personal hygiene was not quite as advanced in those days. The kitchens were supplied from walled gardens covering over 3 acres.

All Saints Church, Eggesford

As an estate chapel, only seating 80 worshippers, the exterior of the building is quite ordinary. The tower, holding three bells is original 14th century, but the rest of the building and its interior were almost completely refurbished in 1878. Nevertheless, the inside is packed with memorials to successive generations of local nobility. They are all around, decorated with coats-of-arms and really enliven the building. As you enter through the north door, The Portsmouth Pew is a box where the choir now sit. The organ, a single keyboard instrument made by Thomas C. Lewis of London, installed in 1948 is also located there. Note the two foot pedals which activate the bellows.

Just outside the front corner of this pew is a pot bellied stove, still plumbed in, that provided the Earl and his family with warmth during winter services. Electricity was not installed until 1965.

The Forestry Commission

Were formed in 1919 as a government agency to take over, manage and initiate woodland planting schemes. Much early work has been criticised in recent years because of their obsession with planting non-indigenous but fast growing conifers. This policy is long past, and they are now sympathetic cultivators of English woodlands, very aware of their responsibilities to the environment and sensitive to the fact that they own vast tracts of countryside. This is manifested by a (relatively) recent policy of positive encouragement to visitors by waymarking walks around their woods.

The woodland on the Eggesford estate was one of their first acquisitions, and the very first tree planted under the régime was here, on this walk, on December 8th 1919.

The Walk

Leave the pub and turn right towards Eggesford station. At the south end, turn right over the level crossing, and along the road. After a couple of hundred yards, take the right-hand turn and walk up the gently rising gradient for about 1 mile before turning right towards The Wembworthy Centre, now owned by Devon Council and hired to schools as a base for exploration and countryside interpretation.

The lane bears left almost immediately, before swinging round to the right. Follow this, and after another 1,000 yards is an entrance on the

"Beware of Cats" near Eggesford Garden Centre. (photo: Elizabeth Fowler)

right with a large sign proclaiming "EGGESFORD FOREST WALK – HEYWOOD FOREST WALK". Take this track. Heywood Forest was first planted in 1920, and has a good mixture of (by now) mature trees.

Ironically, as you pass through the gate and actually enter the forest, the tree-lined walk that has gone before disappears, and you are left in open rolling countryside with super views: Devon at her most glorious. After a short distance, a signpost marked "FOREST WALK" directs you to the right. This leads down a fairly steep slope, a flight of very unevenly spaced steps and arrives at a flat area with a choice of exits. Take the half-left track which continues for a short distance before a right turn descends towards the Taw river.

Almost at the waters edge turn left. Depending of the time of year, this section can really beautiful. There are evergreen laurel bushes waterside for winter greenery, rhododendron for spring and early summer, indigenous deciduous trees for the rest of summer, and a rainbow of exquisite colours in autumn. Tree roots dabble their toes in the water, and it does not take a great leap of imagination to picture the descendants of Tarka snoozing peacefully only a few inches away underfoot, secure in the knowledge that he/she is well-hidden from our prying eyes.

The railway line closes in on the right, and just before it crosses the river on a bridge an un-signposted track to the left heads uphill. Take this, walking away from the river, and as it meets a wider track higher up, turn right, and at the next "T" junction, turn right again. This takes the walk along a relatively level section, hugging the contour as it swings left though almost 180°, around the base of an old Norman motte and bailey castle. This was sited here to control the river ford. It was a Saxon area, with no evidence of any earlier settlement.

The path has now developed into a broad wide track, frequently marked. Cross two roads, and head straight on, along gently rising ground until the walk leaves the trees and ends up back on the road you walked along earlier. You have now completed a loop.

Retrace your steps past the Wemworthy Centre, heading back towards the station. After about half a mile, on the right is a wide driveway. Take this, and follow the track along past a house. On the left is a plaque which marks the site of the first Forestry Commission planting in 1919. The track then turns right alongside the stream before a left turn by the side of a field brings you to a stile into a road. Turn left, and after a few yards the walk comes to a crossroads. Directly ahead is an unpaved path. This is The Tarka Trail (see Walk 11). It is a clearly marked track, the only point of confusion is as it reaches a barn and appears to swing right. The lesser used – straight on – track is the Trail.

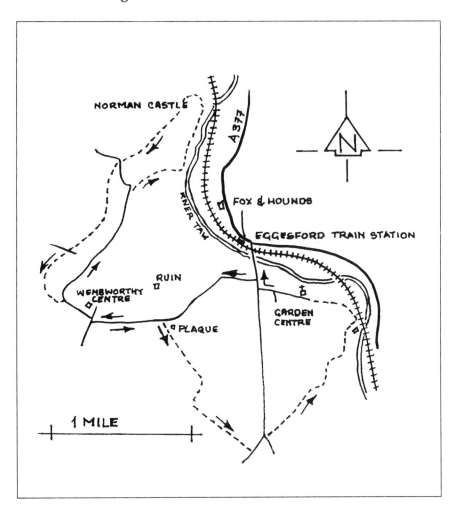

Arriving at Eggesford Barton and a paved road, turn left and walk down the hill to the pretty church. Ahead, on the hill opposite are the ruins of Eggesford House, whilst a drive to the left leads up to Eggesford Garden Centre. At the road, turn right, and the lane leads back to Eggesford station, and, a little further along, The Fox and Hounds.

Walk 13:
Umberleigh – Stowford – Chittlehampton

Lots of ups and downs on this walk, but through lush Devonian scenery with piles of interest en route. The Rising Sun was selected for a starting point because of its proximity to public transport. If this is not a concern, The Bell at Chttlehampton has more to offer. Spring is the ideal time for this walk. The area around Hawkridge woods is carpeted with daffodils, making a wonderful sight.

Distance: 7½ miles.

Terrain: Hilly.

Refreshment: Tearoom in Umberleigh, pub in Chittlehampton, light refreshments at The Cobbaton Combat Collection.

Map: 180.

Grid Reference: SS 608238.

Starting Point: The Rising Sun, Umberleigh, on the A377 Barnstaple to Exeter road. The Bell, Chittlehampton is 2 miles east of Umberleigh.

Transport: BR Umberleigh station within 200 yards.

The Rising Sun Hotel is more of a hotel than pub, but it offers comfortable surroundings in which to enjoy a pint of real ale. The Bell at Chittlehampton has 3 real ales; Boddington's, Bass and one guest beer. Intriguingly, the landlord also stocks no less than 100 varieties of whisky.

The Cobbaton Combat Collection (1)

Opened in 1980 as a tourist attraction, the owner, Preston Isaac has collected military ephemera since he was a child. As he grew older, the size of his purchases grew, and storing items like a 44 ton tank became something of a headache. Eventually the collection got so big he decided to create a showcase so others could enjoy it. What started with a few bullet cases and belt buckles has grown into a comprehensive exposition of wartime equipment and armoured vehicles.

This is very much a "hands-on" museum with exhibits still in battle condition carrying whatever damage they sustained in service: certainly not cleaned and polished. Originally, Preston's interest was in Second World War items, mainly British and Canadian. Now, purchase of land to display his collection has allowed him to diversify into current equipment and post-war Russian and Czechoslovakian armoured vehicles. The replica Horsa glider on display was actually used in filming "A Bridge Too Far". There are Chieftain, Churchill Centaur and T54 tanks, armoured personnel carriers, guns, motor bikes, and scout cars; all the makings of a good old trip down "Memory Lane".

Basic refreshments are available. They are served, in keeping with the tenor of the place, from a 1940 Fordson "V" NAAFI truck. The Cobbaton Combat Collection opens from 9.30am to 6pm every day from April 1st to October 31st, and 9.30am to 4pm November 1st to March 31st on weekdays only

Organised chaos at the Cobbaton Combat Collection. (photo: Elizabeth Fowler)

St Hieritha's Church, Chittlehampton (2)

St Hieritha (or St. Urith) was believed to have been a villager in the 6th century who was converted by visiting missionaries. She devoted herself to a religious life, and as a result was killed by haymakers scythes at the instigation of her stepmother. Where she died, a spring of water bubbled, ending a long drought. The well is no longer in use, but a large stone from it is incorporated into a wall at the east end of Chittlehampton. She was buried in the village and her subsequent Canonization gives the church its unique name. The legend was lost in the mists of time until the discovery of a Latin hymn in a 15th century manuscript at Trinity College Cambridge. This gave the story in graphic detail.

The main entrance is up a delightful avenue of poplar trees, their branches intertwined overhead to create a green canopy. The ornately carved ceiling in the porch has the added attraction of house martins nests, although the droppings from these do not exactly enhance the floor. The church is almost standard Devonian and is interesting without being exciting.

The Walk

Leave the pub and cross the road, over the bridge and past The Gables tea room. On the left is a white building owned by Murch Bros Ltd. As the road turns sharp left, on the left but to the right of the factory is a Public Footpath sign. This leads through a gate and alongside the Taw, under the railway and over a couple of stiles, staying close to the river until you reach a little depression in the ground. Here, move away from the river as the field narrows, with a garden full of bushes to the right, to a gate.

Pass through this gate, and a stile is located in the right-hand hedge some 50 yards along. Up this green lane to the road and turn left, up the hill, past the delightfully named Mousetail Barton, to the crossroads. Straight across is a Public Footpath sign. Head down, over the hill towards the farm in the bottom but keeping it just to the left. Through an orchard to a bridge over Hawkridge Brook and up the steep field beyond where a gate leads into a narrow lane.

Turn left and follow this lane over the brow of a hill and to the Cobbaton Combat Collection (1). Turn right just after this and follow the road to Stowford. At Stowford Cross take the right turn and in Stowford turn right by Polly's Cottage. After 1 mile is a Public Footpath sign on the right. Pass through the gate and keep close to the right-hand hedge. Soon the tower of St. Hieritha's church Chittlehampton (2) hoves into view. Cross the stile into the next field and towards the church. Here the path splits three ways. The right-hand is into the churchyard, and straight ahead leads to the village square with its picture postcard thatched cottages, pump, pub – The Bell, schoolroom and a Wesleyan chapel dated 1858.

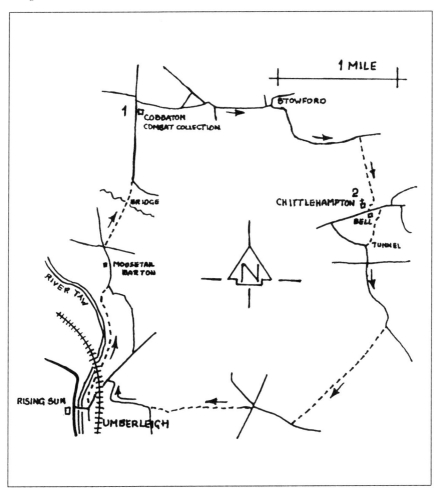

Leave the square in the bottom-left corner (turn right outside The Bell.) A few yards down the road on the right is a Public Footpath sign. Through this gate to a tarmac path, follow this as it winds gently away from the village. Another gate then gives access to a little tunnel under a house to a road. Turn left.

Up the hill is Holmdown Cross where a busy (by Devon standards) road meets the lane. Straight across is the direction, signposted "Chittle-hamholt". The lane drops into a valley and climbs out the other side. As it reaches a sharp left bend, a gateway cut through a bank directly ahead gives access to a Public Footpath. Pass through the next gate and keep the hedge to your right shoulder. At the far end, the stile into the next field is about 30 yards to the left. Into this field, and again keep the hedge to your left shoulder. At the far end a gate gives access to a small cattle holding pen and two exit gates: take the one straight ahead. Another gate leads into the final field of this segment, the exit being just right of straight ahead. At this lane turn right.

Follow this lane to the end and take the left turn. A few yards along, on the right is a Waymark arrow pointing down towards a farm. Soon this drive turns sharp right into the farm buildings, but the walk continues straight ahead into a green lane, and woodland. At a "Y" junction keep to the right-hand (lower) track which leads to a stile into a field. The gate is in the bottom corner which leads into a lane, past a farm and to a surfaced area. Follow this to the road, turn left and the station is a few yards along; the pub just around the corner over the bridge.

If you started at The Bell, as the road turns sharp right, turn right alongside Murch Brothers.

Walk 14:
Around Lundy

This is something spectacularly different: it needs a 2¼ hour sea journey just to get to the start.

Distance: Any distance you want up to 8 miles.

Terrain: Flat, once you have made the steep 400ft ascent from the Landing Beach.

Refreshment: The Marisco Tavern on the island or aboard the ferry.

Map: 180, or a more detailed one of the island on sale aboard the ferry.

Grid Reference: SS 143439.

Starting Point: Either Bideford or Ilfracombe. Details of ferry times from The Lundy Shore Office, The Quay, Bideford, N. Devon EX39 2LY, phone 0237 470422 or fax 0237 477779.

The Marisco Tavern has a wonderfully freebooting feel to it. Maybe it's the imagination, and the fact that you have taken a ship to get there. Or is it the furnishings? They include artifacts from many shipwrecks on the island, and a sign advertising 'Pickled Seagulls Eggs – 1/-' (1/- was a shilling, equivalent to 5p). That certainly reinforces the feeling.

Almost everything on sale comes across on the ferry. And with only a handful of residents, the emphasis is very much on catering for the visitor. The Marisco – including The Tavern Kitchen – is the centre of social life on the island. It opens from 12noon to 2pm and 6pm to 11pm (kitchen until 8.30pm only). There is a good menu and the beers are Barleycorn Pale Ale and Cask Conditioned Dartmoor Bitter.

Lundy

Is from the Old Norse: lundi, which means puffin. It was puffin island to the Danes who used it as a base from which to raid the Devon and Welsh coasts. It had a well-deserved reputation for lawlessness from then until the middle of the eighteenth century. Before the Danes, prehistoric man inhabited the island, leaving behind flint flakes and pottery as evidence of his occupation. Stretching some three miles, it covers roughly 920 acres. The island is fairly flat, some 400ft above sea level with the highest point being Beacon Hill, 471ft.

The pub sign on Lundy, complete with battered navigation light. (photo: Elizabeth Fowler)

The Marisco family were the first documented "baddies" on Lundy. William Morisco (sic) had his story told in graphic detail by Tristram Risdon in the 1630s.

" . . . one William Morisco, conspiring the death of king Henry the third [sometime between 1216 and 1242], at Woodstock, confederated with a knight of the court, to murder him by the inlet of a window into the king's chamber;

But it chanced the king lay elsewhere that night; whereupon the villain sought in other chambers, with the knife drawn in his hand, and found Margaret Bisset, one of the queen's maids, late up, and reading; who much affrighted, made a shrieking noise, and therewith wakened some of the king's servants; they starting up, found, and laid hands onn him, who after some imprisonment, was drawn to pieces at Coventry with horses. Whereupon William Morisco fled, became a pirate, and fortified this island [Lundy], doing much damage to this coast: but at length surprized with sixteen of his accomplices, was put to death."

That was by hanging in 1242. By the early 1600s, the island was once again in the hands of pirate bands who sallied forth into the Bristol Channel to wreak all kinds of mayhem. These days came to an end when a Bideford merchant Thomas Benson MP leased the island. From there, he engaged in his spare time occupation: smuggling. Ownership then passed to W.H.Heaven in 1834, when he paid 9,400 guineas and claimed it as his own independent land, free from the laws of the mainland. It subsequently changed hands several times until the National Trust took over and leased it to The Landmark Trust. They now finance, administer and maintain the island.

There are few buildings, and none of real architectural interest. The remains of Marisco Castle are to be found just south of the hotel. The pleasant Millcombe House, encountered on the walk up from the beach, was built by Mr. Heaven soon after buying the island. It is delightfully sheltered, and has a fine garden with shrubs and trees; one of the few places on the island to be so favoured.

The old lighthouse dates back from 1819, and is now converted for holiday use. The granite tower was built some 90ft tall, but found to be frequently above the cloud base, and thus useless. It was replaced by two new ones, one at each end of the island, built by Trinity House in 1897.

The Ferries

Back in 1879, the first regular supply vessel entered service, albeit carrying very few passengers. As recently as 1985, the *m.v. Polar Bear* only

Lundy ferry MS Oldenberg *awaits passengers fron the island for their return to Bideford*
(photo: Elizabeth Fowler)

carried 12, and prospective visitors had to rely on commercial pleasure ships, or a (very expensive) helicopter service from Hartland Point, which finished in that year. How to increase the arrival of visitors on which the island depended?

The Landmark Trust started searching for a ship able to carry both passengers and cargo, but small enough to cope with shallow water. The *M.S. Oldenberg* was located in Germany. She fitted the bill, was purchased and entered service in May 1986.

The Wildlife

The island is noted for its variety of bird life, both indigenous and migratory. A log is kept in the Marisco Tavern keeping the visitor up to date with most recent sightings. Puffins still nest here, and on the four legged front, sika deer, soay sheep and black rabbits are native. The sea is quite remarkable. There are grey seals, clear blue waters with basking sharks, and rock pools full of magic.

The Walk

How to set about exploring Lundy is essentially a matter of personal choice. Assuming a summer day visit aboard the *M.S. Oldenberg* from Ilfracombe, it could be 1pm or later before getting ashore, leaving less than 3 hours on the island. From Bideford, the return journey is dependant on tides, and can occasionally give 5 hours or more.

The sheer act of arrival on Lundy is different. Forget harbour walls, quays or any such luxury. A small whaleboat will come alongside, sometimes rolling quite alarmingly in the swell. At the precise moment it is lifted by the sea to the level of the unloading door, you step across from the comparative calmness of the Oldenberg. This sounds much more hazardous than it actually is. Sturdy crew members are there to give you a helping hand – literally. They have no wish to blemish their otherwise incident free record. Casting off, dry land is a few roller-coaster yards away. And if you think you're a poor sailor, don't worry. It's exhilarating and over in a few moments, before you have time to even think of being ill.

A steep path leads from the beach to the plateau and village. From there, the nearest thing to a road on the island heads due north for 3 miles to North Light. Alternatively – and much more scenically – there are the

West Sidelands and East Sidelands paths. These follow the edge of the cliffs.

On arriving at the top of the hill, continue to head west along that path which will soon veer right towards the old lighthouse. There are no signposts, but walls known as Quarter, Halfway and Threequarter indicate your whereabouts. Walking to the Halfway wall before turning right, reaching the East Sidelands and turning right again back to the village will give you a three mile walk before sampling the delights of the Marisco Tavern. Or perhaps the north lighthouse appeals. A track runs the full length of the island along the centre, but this is the best part of 7 miles there and back.

You are free to roam pretty well wherever you like, but the rocky inlets clearly hold the greatest attraction.

A Word of Warning

Keep a close eye on your watch, and do not underestimate the time needed to get back to the Landing Beach. You might walk at 3mph on the mainland; you will NOT here, there is just so much to see. And once the ferry has gone, it has gone. Dependant on the time of year it can be up to 10 days before it returns.

Walk 15:
Bickington – Eastacombe – Holywell

Some of this walk is along back lanes on the outskirts of Barnstaple: but you would never know it. Peace and pretty scenery rule and there are some stunning views en route. If you are able, time your departure to around 3 hours before high tide. This will add to your enjoyment by providing a full river for the last section, rather than muddy banks that are visible at low water.

Distance: 8 miles.

Terrain: Quite hilly, but not too steep.

Refreshment: Start/finish only. A shop and Chinese takeaway by Barnstaple Bridge.

Map: 180.

Grid Reference: SS 530326.

Starting Point: The Old Barn, Bickington, which is on the B3233 Barnstaple to Bideford road.

Transport: Barnstaple to Bideford 'bus services stop close to the door. Enquiries on 01271 382800. These buses also stop very close to the train station at Barnstaple.

The Old Barn has an attractive "olde worlde" look about it from the outside with its low thatched roof. But it started life as a small building this century and has been added to piecemeal over the years. The inside has suffered to a degree from the depredations of brewery refurbishment as passing trade increased. Until the North Devon link road was built at the end of the 1980s, this was the A39, a main holiday route and eternally busy with traffic. Now it relies on a more settled trade, and to that end offers a good selection of draught ales with always 2 "guest beers" available. At the time of my visit, one was "Speckled Hen". Worthington and Bass are also available on a regular basis. The place is open 11.30 – 2.30 and from 5pm every day except Sunday when national rules apply.

Barnstaple Bridge

As discussed in Walk 7, Barnstaple's *raison d'etre* was the lowest crossing place on the river Taw. The exact date of the first bridge construction is unsure, but it is believed to have been around 1200. It was built of stone and contained 16 arches with spans of up to 22ft, but was only about 9ft wide; suitable for pedestrians and pack horses only. Widening took place in 1796 and 1832. When the railway was constructed in 1873, the south end had to be re-aligned to accommodate the iron railway bridge.

The "castle" overlooking the Taw estuary. The main body is newly built.(photo: Elizabeth Fowler)

Known as The Long Bridge of Barnstaple, its original funding is obscure, but it was administered for over 700 years by a Trust who maintained it – toll free – until 1961 when the Ministry of Transport assumed responsibility.

To the left (downstream) of the bridge, but very close, the railway used to cross on its way to Ilfracombe. There was a wheel-screechingly sharp bend towards the other end as the line turned left to gain Barnstaple Town station. That was the interchange for the Lynton and Barnstaple Railway (See Walk 1). The radius of the curve was such that only selected steam engines could get round it.

The Walk

Leave the pub and turn right, walking towards an Evoco filling station. Just before reaching it, there is a lane to the right. Take this, and follow the path through to some bungalows, and on to a "T" junction. Directly opposite is a footpath which leads to a stile and then a bridge over a stream. Ahead is a long but fairly narrow field. Aim for roughly the centre of the far hedge and there is the stile that leads into a country lane. Turn left and immediately right into a lane marked No Through Road.

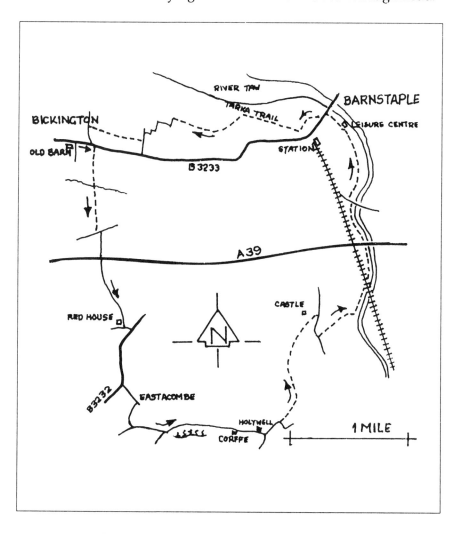

At the end is the busy A39 road carrying high speed traffic. Cross with care and take the lane directly opposite, signposted "Brynsworthy". This is a long uphill climb, but after only a few minutes the frenetic pace of life on the A39 is behind and relative tranquillity returns. Pause during the ascent and turn to admire the view. On the left, Westward Ho! and the sweep of the Taw river to the whole of Barnstaple and Exmoor beyond. Breathtaking: in more ways than one!

At the next road junction by an attractive B & B called Red House, turn left and then right on reaching the next road a few yards along at Rowdon Barton. This carries more traffic than most roads used on these walks, and there is no footpath, so care is needed for the 500 yards or so involved before a left turn to Eastacombe returns the walk to its accustomed peace. Follow this lane through the village taking the "Tawstock" sign at each divergence.

Eastacombe Evangelical Chapel, a brightly painted building constructed in 1818 is on the left, and the disused Templeton Quarry creates a sheer drop to the right. The road then starts to drop quite rapidly into a valley. On the right is a very tasteful development at Corffe whilst on the left is a school with thatched buildings – most unusual and attractive. Take the left turn which also acts as drive for the school. This is Holywell, and the source of the name is under a tree to the left.

Ahead, to the left of the white village hall is a footpath sign which points to the right over a stile. Cross the field, keeping to the high side of a ridge, and the exit stile is partially concealed by shrubbery. Over the stile, into woodland and to a parting of the ways beneath an electricity pylon; take the left, which leads uphill. Eventually, the climb steepens, bears to the left and passes through a gate with a new house just to the right. Follow the perimeter fence and the driveway leading to this house will be the walk.

Directly ahead, on the skyline is a rather imposing castle. Regrettably, it is nothing of the kind, most of the building is quite new. But the towers are original. The view from the top is over the estuary, and local rumour – not backed by hard evidence, is that the original was constructed in the 14thC. The only documents immediately to hand date the place as late 18thC. It is currently being finished out as a private residence, and will command views that are probably unsurpassed locally. However, with its position, exposed to the elements, the heating bill will probably exceed the average mortgage.

On reaching the end of the drive turn right, down the hill, and after

300 yards, take a left, marked "Public Footpath". Keep to the contour, and across the field is a stile which leads almost down the river, and then begins another climb along a quite rough track which leads to the banks of the Taw.

Turn left. The route is now along the bank of the river, first under a railway, then a road bridge to a disused railway bridge. This used to give the Great Western Railway Taunton to Barnstaple line access to Barnstaple Junction station and the Ilfracombe and Bideford routes. Just underneath, move slightly to the left where a paved path continues the walk.

Arriving at huge white building – North Devon Leisure centre – keep to the left and gain the road which leads to a traffic island. Cross the road. Opposite is a large white brick building which is the N.T. Shapland and Petter works. Here, a short detour is advised. Just a few yards to the right is Barnstaple Bridge.

Return to Shapland and Petter's and take the road to the left-hand side of their works, which is signposted "Country Park and Coast Path – Bideford". This road curves quite sharply to the left before turning right. The walk continues straight ahead. This was the bed of the Barnstaple to Ilfracombe railway (see Walk 3), a fact evidenced by the disused bridge arch that appears in view shortly.

Turn right just before the bridge, through a kissing gate and pick up The Tarka Trail. This heads towards Instow and Bideford. About half a mile along, there is a small bridge over a footpath, beneath some power lines. Take the track that turns half left to join that other footpath in a dip, walking away from the river and uphill to a fork; take the right-hand path. As the climb finishes with a sharp left-hand bend, bear right along the back of housing before turning left, between two houses, through a gate and onto an estate. Take the road opposite (Park Avenue) which soon reaches a junction; turn right into Lynhurst Avenue.

This road soon reaches a dead end, but there is a left turn into Oakland Park South. The culs-de-sac on each side are all part of the same road, so the turn you seek is third right, which contains housing numbered 38 – 44. At the end of here is a Public Footpath sign which immediately turns left followed by a sharp right which leads to a "T". Turn left and then take the Public Footpath sign which is shortly to be found on the right. A Gate soon appears to bar the way, but a narrow path to the right-hand side takes the walk past more housing, over a stile and at the next junction of paths, turn left through the farmyard. This leads to the main road, where a right turn leads back to the pub, just 100 yards away.

Walk 16:
Instow – Knightacott – Fremington

The unspoilt seaside village of Instow lies on the Torridge river where it joins the Taw and flows out to sea. Although attracting holidaymakers, there are no amusements/candy floss/bingo halls. This results in a visitor who enjoys the surroundings, rather than a determined pursuit of pleasure. A west-facing beach, yachting and wind-surfing on the water and a remarkable cricket ground provide endless entertainment. The scoreboard at the latter is the only thatched one in the country, and a six-hit can land in the sea. The Royal Marines exercise in the estuary, providing free entertainment with DUKW's, Landrover's and small lorries plunging into the sea to load themselves aboard waiting landing craft.

Distance: 8 miles.

Terrain: 1 steep hill at the start.

Refreshment: Plenty in Instow and Fremington.

Map: 180.

Grid Reference: SS 473307.

Starting Point: The Wayfarer Inn, just off the seafront in Lane End Road, Instow. Instow lies between Barnstaple and Bideford on the B3233. Short term parking on the seafront, long term 150 yards from the pub.

Transport: Good 'bus service between Barnstaple and Bideford. Details of 01271 382800

The Wayfarers has been a pub for over 100 years. It was converted from 3 old cottages which are believed to date back to the 16th century. An excellent range of food and bar snacks are always avalaible and, as a free house with a landlord who is *au fait* with his customers needs, there's a constantly changing cellar with never less than 4 real ales. Furnishings are good, the company convivial, and there is a skittle alley out in the back where the local team strives for success. Not always a star performer, but a team member is David Shepherd, the world class cricket umpire.

Fremington [3]

If you were asked to list ports in order of volume of trade, Fremington is not the name that would immediately spring to mind. Yet, with the coming of the railway in 1854, trade flourished. Coal arrived by coaster from south Wales, for onward movement by rail, whilst wagonloads of clay from Peters Marland were loaded for shipment all around the world. In its heyday, it handled larger tonnages than any port between Lands End and Bristol. Those days are now history. The railway is gone, and the ships no longer call.

A group of walkers pause at Fremington Quay on the Taw estuary. The hills beyond are the location of walk 7. (photo: Elizabeth Fowler)

A busy pottery was also located in the village. Started in the 1790s by George Fishley, it passed through several generations of the family before being sold to Brannam's in Barnstaple who closed it in 1914. Their main output was larger storage vessels such as pitchers, bread jars and meat pickling pans. The firm won several awards in the 1800s for the quality of their decorative work, and were pioneers in colouring local clay.

Ball Clay

Clay has been dug from the Peters Marland area to the south for centuries. The earliest records of extraction go back to 1680. It was well-established in 1827 when the Rolle Canal was opened (see Walk 20). Prior to that event, clay used to move (very slowly) to Bideford by horse and cart. With the opening of the canal to Torrington, the road journey was cut in half. Its main use is in the pottery industry, its light colour after firing making it very popular with potters. It was also used to make bricks locally, a fact evidenced by the preponderance of cream/white fronted houses. Today, it is exported to continental Europe – Spain being a regular destination – through the port of Bideford.

The Sand Barges [7]

Much of the sand and gravel needed by local builders comes from the estuary. Sea dredged aggregate as it is known has been gathered for years, primarily by Barum Sand and Gravel Ltd. From their quay beside the river Yeo in Barnstaple two barges, the *Marlene Grace* and *Louise Grace* leave at high tide to cruise down the river to Crow Point, opposite Instow. There they are beached on the ebbing tide and abandoned until the water starts to rise again. Then, a loading shovel appears from behind the lighthouse and scoops some 60 tons of sand from alongside, into the holds. The covers are replaced and secured ready for off as the incoming tide re-floats them. From afar, this can appear extremely disconcerting as the barges drop from sight in any choppy water.

Then, lying so low in the water that the gunwales and deck are awash, they make their way back up the river to arrive at the top of the tide, turn into the narrow entrance of the Yeo, tie up and discharge opposite Rolle Quay (see Walk 7)

The Walk

The thrombosis-inducing hill is right at the start of this walk. Leave the pub and turn left along the seafront to the first left turn which is Kiln Close Lane. At the top, turn left and just across the road is a flight of steps and a Public Footpath sign. This is Millards Hill. Pause halfway up (you'll probably be glad of the rest) and look back. There are scintillating views out over the estuary towards Lundy, 20 miles away in the Bristol Channel, but often visible.

Over a stile at the top and the field leads to a narrow lane. Turn left; right at the end and follow this to the "T" junction. Turn right. A couple of hundred yards along there is a left turn [2] that is not signposted, but is through the gate of Beacon Farm. At the end of the next field are two stiles. Both will get you to Knightacott Farm, but the one directly ahead is also used by a spring, and can be very muddy. It is also extremely overgrown in summer. Pass by the farm, following the narrow lane. As it meets a road, directly across is the entrance to Brake Plantations. This is a pretty wooded area with a stream through the valley bottom. It was once dammed for a mill that used to exist a little further downstream.

Out of the wood, the path runs along the edge of a field before reaching a road. Here, turn right, cross the stream and at the next junction turn left. This brings you to the main road. Shops, toilets and pubs are to the right; a largish supermarket and a chemist to the left up the hill. Cross the road diagonally left, and a path to the left of the stream leads past the large nursing home that used to be an army base, and to the estuary. Pass through the gate at the end and turn left to continue the walk. Seats and a table are provided just to the right; a place to pause and admire the

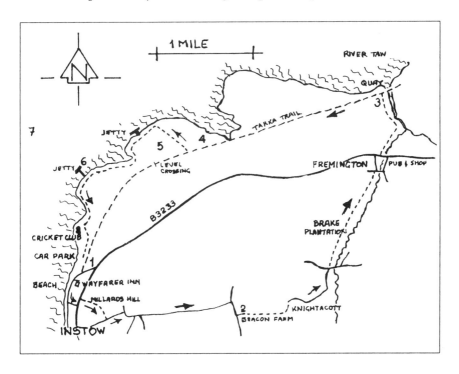

esturial view. This is Fremington Quay [3]. A memorial stone notes the death of a local in 1986, and there are usually lots of seabirds and waders around when the tide is right.

Heading south west now, the level walking is along the course of an old railway. This was the Bideford to Torrington (and later Halwill Junction see Walk 20) railway, a victim of the Beeching cuts and closed to passengers in 1965, but continuing to carry ball clay from Meeth until 1982. At the second turn on the right, at the end of Islay Nature Reserve [4] (another fine place for birds), there is a choice of routes. Straight ahead, over an old level crossing and past the Royal Marines base [1], there is a gap in the hedge on the right with one step up. Through there is the main car park. If you have parked on the seafront, walk up to the road and turn right.

Of far more interest is the right turn. Cross the stile towards the Taw river. After 100 yards, ignore the waymark arrow which indicates a right turn, and carry straight on. Underfoot, the ground has turned somewhat ashy. This used to be Yelland Power Station [5], and the by-product was spread around this site. The path bears to the left and passes a jetty where coal from south Wales collieries was once unloaded.

Along a ridge, with marshland to the left and estuary to the right, this is another fine place for seabird life. A wide variety of duck often gather here in the winter. Widgeon and pochard are frequently seen along with the ubiquitous mallard. The next jetty is Yelland Oil Terminal [6]. Here small tankers regularly discharge up to 1200 tons of petroleum products into the waiting tanks. The ships, which cross from the refinery at Milford Haven in South Wales, are just a few yards away, the sole shipping movement left on the Taw. The only other commercial trafic are a few inshore fishing boats and the sand barges, although ships for Bideford enter the estuary before turning right into the Torridge.

Beyond the jetty, the path is extremely undulating though a series of sand dunes. It is possible to walk along the beach, which is usually more pleasant. At the end of this beach, take the flight of steps over the boulders to the left, walk up the lane with the cricket ground [8] to the right and follow this track back to the main road. At low tides, you can stick to the beach, cross a rocky outcrop to the main Instow beach and walk along until the sand dunes finish, at which point, head left towards the road, and a gap in the sea wall will bring you out at your starting point.

Walk 17:
Westleigh – Eastleigh – Ball Hill

Westleigh is a pretty village on the eastern slopes of the Torridge with a splendid pub. The walk is through typically undulating Devonian terrain and the greenest of green lanes.

Distance: 4 miles.

Terrain: Gently undulating.

Refreshment: Only the pub at the start/finish.

Map: 180.

Grid Reference: SS 472287.

Starting Point: The Westleigh Inn, Westleigh, just east of the B3233 Barnstaple to Bideford road.

Transport: Westleigh has no public transport, but the Bideford to Barnstaple services operate on the B3233 half a mile west of the pub.

The pub is a friendly place with a good local trade swelled by visitors, particularly on summer weekends when the garden is packed. The menu is extensive and very good value, the beer a little less imaginative. Ruddles is augmented by Ushers Triple Crown and John Smiths, Guinness, but no real cider. Hours are 11.30am to 2.30pm and 6pm to 11pm.

Sir Mike Ansell

Sir Michael Picton Ansell, who died in 1994, was one of this area's most celebrated residents. He was the man who ran the Horse of the Year Show in London from 1949 until 1975, and saw it established as a major equestrian event on the world calender. During this time (1963 to 1972) he was also Chairman of The British Showjumping Association: and all this whilst blind.

During the early months of 1940, he was a Lieutenant-Colonel in the 1st Lothian and Border Yeomanry with the British Expeditionary Force in France. He was wounded and taken prisoner, and those wounds eventually caused him to lose his sight. Lack of sight never daunted him, and he continued to enjoy his life to the full. He adored fishing, and pottered about in his beautifully maintained garden almost to the end. He was Knighted for his services to equestrianism in 1968.

Aiming to draw custom from the nearby main road, The Westleigh Inn sign points into the village. Across the estuary is West Appledore (Walk 18) and the hills above Braunton (Walk 6). (photo: Elizabeth Fowler)

The Walk

Leave the car park and turn left, down to the main(?) road, and turn left again, heading towards the church which is on the left. The cricket ground just beyond, on the same side is in an exquisite location. It must be a somewhat difficult playing area with a pronounced Lords type slope down which the ball gathers speed as it races towards the boundary. The esturial view from the ground is, again, wonderful.

Immediately past the ground, on the right is a gate with a Public Footpath sign. The walk heads over a stile into a field. After the stile at the next fence, head diagonally left towards the corner of the field where yet another stile leads into a track alongside a house, once the local school, to a 'T' junction. Turn left. Soon after, this road swings to the right; the walk follows the lesser road to the left.

300 yards along this road, hard by a gnarled oak tree, a stile on the right gives access to a Public Footpath. This is seldom used, and in summer presents a formidable obstacle of brambles, stinging nettles and thistles. It leads to a rustic bridge over a stream before tracking diagonally left up the embankment at the top of which is a main road. Across

this is another Public Footpath sign pointing diagonally left up the hill. A small gate through more nettles gives access to the next field. This is regularly used for arable crops, so walk the perimeter to the right. At the far end, a gate gives access to Eastleigh Manor.

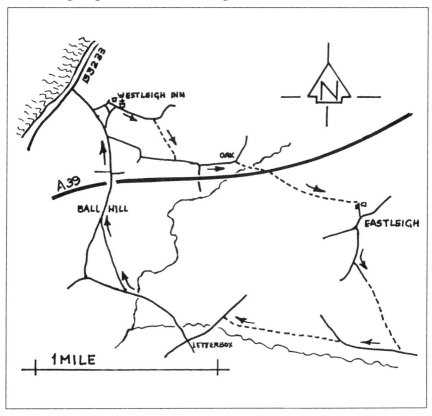

In the farm yard, note the old grain store standing on round stone pillars. Turn right by this and walk to the road at the end. The house on the left here was once the farm foreman's cottage and had a thatched roof. One day during the mid 1940s it caught fire and was gutted. The house there now is a rebuild from that disaster. To the left, an old milestone informs "BARUM 6 MILES; an old local abbreviation for Barnstaple.

Turn right past the old village blacksmith's shop. Another row of cottages to the right were also once occupied by farm workers, and for many years in the 1940s and 50s had two "ladies" in adjacent houses who hated the sight of each other. They were given to regular bouts of fisticuffs on the stone forecourts, and the farmer was frequently called to split them up; often at great personal risk. Around the corner from this row are two further dwellings. Side by side, they are named Joy Cottage and Folly Cottage.

Take the left turn on the bend, leaving the hamlet of Eastleigh and some 400 yards along, follow a signposted track to the left. Starting as a good path, this also eventually deteriorates into something of a struggle against the undergrowth: but not for long. At the road, turn right. As this narrow lane turns right and uphill, take the Public Footpath sign to the left. This leads through a gate into a field with a hill ahead and a wood and stream to the left. Walk parallel with the stream and a gate gives access into another field which leads into a dip and out onto a road. Turn left. Only a few yards along here is a crossroads with a small letter box to the left. Turn right. This was home ground for the late Mike Ansell. As this road heads uphill, take the right turn with a small sign indicating Rose Mill. At the top, turn right, then pause awhile to drink in the view over Appledore and Irsha (Walk 18), Crow Point, and Saunton Sands.

As you cross the bridge that takes you back over the new road, the view to the left of Bideford and the elegant concrete bridge striding out over the river is a delightful one. On reaching the housing that is Westleigh, turn left at the next junction, walk past the thatched Rock Cottage built about 1560, before turning right. At the end of this lane, the road opposite will lead back to the car park.

Walk 18:
Irsha

You will not find the name "Irsha" on your map; look for West Appledore. Official nomenclature notwithstanding, many locals, particularly the older ones, still prefer its original name. This is the shortest walk in the book, never out of sight of housing, but crammed with interest.

Distance: 2½ miles.

Terrain: No severe gradients, but one short drag to the 160ft contour.

Refreshment: Appledore has a range of restaurants, pubs, cafés, shops and fast food outlets.

Map: 180.

Grid Reference: SS 464306.

Starting Point: The Car Park at the north end of the quay. There are a couple of spaces outside The Royal George, but effectively, there is no parking in West Appledore (Irsha).

Transport: Buses to Bideford and Barnstaple.

Because of parking problems, we start this walk in a car park. The Beaver Inn and The Royal George are within a few yards of each other about half a mile into the walk. They have both been adapted somewhat to cater for holidaymakers and their families rather than smugglers, fishermen and wreckers who once made up their clientèle. Both offer a real ale and food.

The Champion of Wales, near the end is a more basic pub, and does not have the range of beers. But what is does have almost next door is a wet fish shop that has recently diversified into fish and chips, owned by a man who also operates fishing boats. What he catches is on sale, fish so fresh it's almost flapping! Individual orders are cooked whilst you wait, and there are often types of fish offered that you will never come across anywhere else; a super establishment.

The Moviemakers In Irsha

An apocryphal (?) story illustrates the somewhat individual looks of the locals. In the 1950s a film crew arrived to make a swashbuckler. Extras were needed to crew the pirate ship. The director sent out his assistant to recruit, and on the appointed day, the ship (built in the estuary by Hinks) was manned. The director congratulated the make-up artist for managing to make them look so villainous. That worthy declaimed: "But I did nothing. It's their natural appearance".

The Beaver Inn alongside the sea wall at West Appledore (Irsha).(photo: Alison Fowler).

Appledore

There has been settlement in these parts since the 11th century when Tawmouth is recorded. The hill behind the village is said to be the site of a battle in 1069 when three of King Harold's illegitimate sons landed an army from over 60 ships to take on the Normans. They were repulsed. Bloody Corner (SS 455293) is reputed to be the site of the conflict.

Shipbuilding has been a major occupation here for centuries. That great Elizabethan seadog Sir Richard Grenville owned much of the land hereabouts, and fitted out ships in the estuary. That industry has now virtually died, although Appledore Shipbuilders still keep the flag flying. They used to be located just upstream of the quay at Richmond, but are now a little further along at Bidna, there operating the largest undercover shipbuilding facility in Europe where vessels up to 2,000 tons are still constructed. Launching is somewhat mundane compared to the spectacular methods at other shipyards. The vast doors to the shed are opened, along with the floodgates, and as the tide rises, out floats the ship, controlled by 2 tugs brought down from Avonmouth (Bristol) for the occasion. Final fitting of masts and so on is carried out at a quay a few yards down the river.

Appledore Quay. Improved sea defences have altered the quay, but the buildings have changed little in the 75 years or so since this picture was taken.

Appledore Lifeboat Station (3)

Because of tidal problems, launching a full-sized lifeboat from here is not possible and the boat is left permanently afloat. When an emergency call is received, a small dingy stored inside the lifeboat house ferries the crew to the boat. An inshore rescue craft is also kept in the station, together with a list of operations carried out over the years. It is usually open in the summer, and on Sundays in the winter. A few souvenirs are on sale, supporting the sterling work still carried out by the RNLI. Sunday morning is often a good time to visit.

If the tide is right, this is practice day, and both boats fly around the estuary simulating rescues. Until its closure at the end of 1994, helicopters from RAF Chivenor, across the water occasionally turned out for joint training. Men would be winched up and down, in and out of the water; all excellent spectator entertainment, notwithstanding its more serious side.

The Walk

Leave the car park and turn right, past St. Mary's parish church on the left. The first road to the right is Irsha Street. This is the direction of the walk, but the first short detour lies ahead.

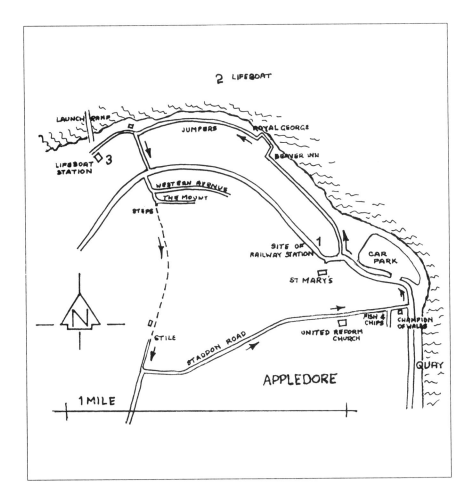

A few yards along the main road turns to the right into Richmond Street. The brick wall on the right is all that remains of Appledore railway station (1 & See Walk 19). The smoke blackened wall is where the waiting room fire once burnt.

Return to Irsha Street, a narrow one-way street with traffic coming from behind you. Quaint is the only adjective that fits. Crazy angles, scant reference to any building line, a riot of colours, the houses that crowd into the street are thoroughly individualistic, showing that todays planning conformity is nothing to do with order, and another example of the glory that can be achieved without planners. Even the camber of the road is at odds with normality. Rainwater runs to the centre where a narrow channel, still cobbled, connects with the drains.

A sharp right, after the houses on the right finish, takes the road down alongside the sea wall and The Beaver Inn. There is no beach, just a rocky outcrop, with the Appledore lifeboat (2) moored in the centre of the channel. The Royal George is a signal for housing on the right again, and the road turns left and right to accommodate it. There are dozens of pretty terraces, secret alleyways and passages that demand exploration. Much of the interest in this place needs uncovering, rather than being there on display.

A shop behind an ordinary door on the left for instance. Here you can still buy "Irsha" pattern fishermen's knit jumpers. Years ago, each fishing village knitted its own particular style, and the fisherman's home port could be deduced from the jumper he wore. On the occasions that bodies were pulled from the sea, this simple form of identification, in the days of almost universal illiteracy, was invaluable.

The housing ends again, and a footpath runs alongside the sea wall, offering good views out into the estuary. Mooring buoys are provided here for any boats who require refuge in this sheltered water. The walk turns left, but the second detour of a few yards gives an opportunity to view the lifeboat station (3). The houses around here are redolent of a different age: Old Coastguards, Old Custom House.

Back to the walk. At the top of the street is a main road. Turn right and immediately left up Western Avenue. 100 yards along, take the right-hand fork up The Mount, and on the right is a steep flight of steps with a Public Footpath sign. These lead to a stile. Cross this and head generally right towards a white house. At the top of the rise, pause a moment, turn round and absorb the incredible view. Across the estuary are the sand-hills of Braunton Burrows, below are Northam Burrows, a wildlife sanctuary, and a rusty old building on the shoreline was the yacht and boat builders J. Hinks and Son until closure, and beyond, the white houses of Westward Ho!

Pass the house to the left, cross the stile onto a paved path, and beyond is Staddon Road. Turn left, through some quite pleasant modern housing before the road plunges downhill into Appledore, past the gaunt United Reform Church, and The Champion of Wales pub. At the junction, turn left to the car park.

Walk 19:
Abbotsham – Westward Ho! –
Greencliff

Coastal scenery, rolling hills and pretty lanes with North Devon's leading tourist attraction at the end. What a mixture.

Distance: 6 miles.

Terrain: No severe gradients.

Refreshment: Pub near Pusehill only. Bradicks in Westward Ho! is close to the walk.

Map: 180.

Grid Reference: SS425265.

Starting Point: The Thatched Inn, Abbotsham, just off the A39 Bideford to Bude trunk road.

Transport: Rudimentary service to Bideford.

The name gives it away; another thatched pub. This one is over 400 years old, and has a good line in real ales: Butcombe and Courage Directors are always available. Cidermaster and Scrumpy Jack are also on draught: for those who dare! There is a lunchtime and evening menu, and the place is open from 11am to 3pm and 6pm to 11pm in summer, a little less in winter.

The Bideford, Westward Ho! And Appledore Railway [1]

With a lifespan of just 16 years, this line hardly registered in the longevity stakes, but the existence of much photographic evidence, some infrastructure, and traces of its course offers an intriguing study.

It was built very late in the railway age, fighting a losing battle with roads from the start. It was 7 miles long and had no physical connection with the LSWR station which, although named Bideford, was actually sited at East-the-Water on the opposite side of the Torridge river. The new line took a horribly circuitous route to Westward Ho! and later, Appledore, whilst the local horse drawn omnibuses which called at the main line station, went much more directly; and cheaply. It was a very determined passenger who would leave the London and South Western

Railway train, walk over the bridge to the BWHAR on the Quay and pay double the fare just to ride on another train.

Construction work started in mid 1898, and the opening from Bideford to Westward Ho! was celebrated on April 24th 1901. Originally planned as a narrow (3ft) gauge line, the promoters, hoping perhaps for an eventual link with the main line, changed to standard gauge before construction was started. The Appledore extension was not completed until May 1st 1908.

Upon completion, there were three intermediate stations, and eight halts: all in seven miles! The station in Westward Ho! was quite a grand affair for such a small line. Along with the platforms there was a buffet, bookstall and waiting room and a large hall built for entertainments of the seaside variety.

The Company was in difficulties from the very start. The local council objected continuously to a railway running along Bideford quay, a busy road where ships were always unloading. Officials fought a long battle, damning virtually every move the company made.

This constant attrition, coupled with a complete lack of profitability saw the curtain fall on March 28th 1917: with an unusual final act. All the track and locomotives were requisitioned by the government for use in the battlefields of Flanders. Removal of the locos caused considerable headaches and much entertainment for the populace. The only way to move them was over the ancient road bridge across the river to East-the-Water where they could transfer to the main line.

In July, track was laid along the length of the quay towards the bridge. Curve and gradient combined to make a left turn onto the bridge an impossible manoeuvre. The rails were then arranged to make a right turn into Bridge Street. From there, the locos could reverse over the bridge.

There were three tank engines operating, each having a name with local connotations. Torridge, after the river, Kingsley, after writer Charles, author of "The Water Babies", and Grenville, a family of seafarers, of which, Sir Richard, a contemporary of Raleigh was the most famous.

The fate of two of the engines has given birth to an fascinating local legend. They were rumoured to have been loaded for France aboard a ship sunk by torpedo off Padstow (Cornwall). The veracity of this was doubted because no official records could be found to confirm the sinking. However, recent discovery by scuba divers of a wreck off the port re-opened speculation when an apparent cargo of railway materials was reported. The third locomotive was broken up for scrap in the 1930s.

An inspirationally(?) named Thatched Inn at Abbotsham.(photo: Elizabeth Fowler).

Bideford Black

This is a seam of very poor grade anthracite coal which runs in a narrow band for some 15 miles from Greencliff to Bideford – where it was mined at East-The-Water – and inland. Its poor burning quality meant the fuel was in greater demand as a pigment. But the fact that it was close to the surface and available saw it used locally.

The Big Sheep

A few yards from the pub is a delightful farm, The Big Sheep. Unashamedly a tourist attraction, it is none the less interesting for that, winning many local and national awards, and featured regularly on television. Julie and Mike Turner have turned a 400 acre mixed farm into an exposition of sheep farming, but with the accent on entertainment. Daily demonstrations of shearing, milking and dog handling are all fun, but subordinate to the main attraction: Sheep Racing.

With knitted woollen jockeys, the sheep race along the course secure in the knowledge that a good feed awaits them. With delightfully punnish names: Sheargar, Red Ram, and Aldernitty, the "race" is presided over by Richard Turner. His build-up is jaw-achingly funny, full of wit and sparkle, whilst the actual commentary equals anything the TV horserace pundits achieve for intensity of excitement. There is always a good range of "sheepy" products on sale. The ice cream is particularly delicious; well recommended, as is the whole event.

St. Helen's Church Abbotsham [6]   -

Attractive in a rugged sort of way, this corner of the village reflects life as it used to be. Attached to the very well-maintained graveyard is the old schoolroom, and an archway giving access to the church. The present school was rebuilt in 1851 " . . . at the sole expence (*sic*) of W.C.Haywood Esq., MD of Kenwith in this Parish."

The Walk

Turn left from the pub, walk down to a "T" junction and bear left. There is a wide grass verge alongside this road, which is a little busier than is usual in Devon. Beyond Whitehouse Cross, the road climbs a small hill and drops down the other side before bearing off to the right. The walk takes the much less used left turn signposted "Pusehill". A couple of yards before the junction, note the rusty blue gate on the right, and a track into a field on the left [1]. Here was where the Bideford, Westward Ho! and Appledore Railway crossed.

The lane heads gently uphill before reaching a "T" junction. Directly across the road, between two houses is a door in a high fence. The Public Footpath goes through here and starts a gentle descent towards the sea, now visible properly for the first time. These are Kipling Tors [2], and are in the care of The National Trust. The going underfoot is rocky, and care is needed, especially when the ground is wet.

As the path turns left and get steeper, pause for a moment to drink in the panorama. The locals say that if you can see Lundy clearly it is going to rain. If you can't, it is raining. One must be very poor of spirit not to perform an involuntary intake of breath at the sheer majesty of the view. In fact the only blight is when your eyes drop down to below your feet at serried ranks of caravans which add to the overall impression not one jot.

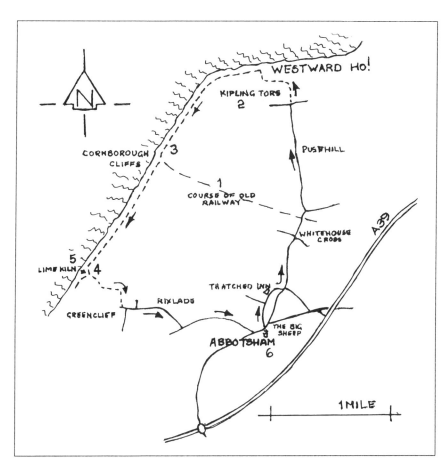

Almost at the foot of the Tor, the path turns right, passes through a barrier of upright railway sleepers and heads down a broken tarmac path alongside the caravans to a somewhat decrepit but interesting large house on the edge of the shore. There are toilets here. Turn left, taking the wide well-made path which climbs gently and is signposted "Coast Path". This was the original route of the railway [1]. At a point towards the top of the hill [3], there used to be a station, Cornborough Halt, built with not a single habitation in sight; it could not have been over-used.

Soon after the top of the gradient, the old railway curves sharp left, whilst the path bears to the right. By now, the exquisite views on offer around here are revealed in all their glory. The vistas from the top of Kipling Tor might be more expansive, but the mass of Hartland now dominates. The white houses of Clovelly, clinging to the steep hillside are easy to pick out from here.

The path continues along in a generally south westerly direction before making a short detour inland to cross a shallow gorge on a wooden footbridge [4]. Here, the waymark arrow indicates a right turn, but there is a stile to the left with another arrow. This is the walk. As you cross the bridge, look down into the ravine on the right. There is a small ruin [5] on the cliff edge. Unlikely as it seems, this was a lime kiln. And an even more unlikely fact is that it was fired with local coal, Bideford Black

There is a path down to the shore here, where ships laden with limestone and culm used to be sewed. A Dictionary of Devonian is needed to translate that. It simply means that the ships came in with the tide, and were left high and dry when it receded. They were then unloaded, and the cargoes transported up the hill to the kiln.

Having turned inland, the walk now makes its way gently uphill through a narrow band of scrub between two fields. There are newly planted trees which will, in time, add to the overall picture of bucolic England. At the next stile head generally in a straight line, keeping the fence to the left about 50 yards away. As the climb levels off, there is a gate directly ahead, with a fence and stile just to the right. Cross the stile and walk towards Greencliff farm where yet another stile drops the walk into a lane. Turn left.

Follow this lane through the settlement at Rixlade and to a "T" junction. Turn left, and half a mile later you will reach the centre of Abbotsham. Turn left. There is a Post Office and shop just around the corner and the church of St.Helen's to the right. Beyond the church, is a crossroads. Take the left-hand turn down an un-named road, past The Old Vicarage and back to The Thatched Inn with its straw pheasant atop the roof.

Walk 20:
Torrington Station – Frithelstock – Monkleigh

The start and finish of this amble around inland Devon uses the Tarka Trail, making walking easy whilst offering a wide variety of scenery.

Distance: 8 miles.

Terrain: Undulating with only one fairly steep climb.

Refreshment: Pub and garage shop in Monkleigh, pub in Frithelstock.

Map: 180.

Grid Reference: SS 480198.

Starting Point: The Puffing Billy, alongside the A386 Bideford to Torrington road.

Transport: Torrington to Bideford bus service.

The buiding now housing The Puffing Billy was constructed by the London and South Western Railway Company in 1871 as their station for Great Torrington. It was converted in 1983, soon after the railway finally left the area. It's a warm, friendly family pub, with roaring open wood fires in winter. There is a restaurant for full meals, and bar snacks as well, "own brand" Puffing Billy bitter, brewed by Ind Coope, together with Dartmoor and Burton beers. There is also a variety of ciders including Scrumpy Jack. NOT recommended before a walk.

The Rolle (or Torrington) Canal

North Devon is an unlikely setting for a canal, but in the early days of the nineteenth century road travel was almost impossible. Farmers more than a few miles from the coast could not obtain fertiliser for their land, or distribute their produce. Lord John Rolle, owner of thousands of Devon acres, employed a local engineer James Green to survey a possible line for a canal to connect Torrington with the sea. That would allow limestone from South Wales to be brought inland, burnt and distributed to a much wider area. Construction was started in 1823 and the eight mile line opened in 1827.

It was an unusual canal in that it used very small boats known as tubs. Each one carried about 5 tons, and they were hauled in trains of three by horses. The limestone arrived in Appledore or Bideford and was trans-shipped into barges. They operated up the Torridge as far as the start of the canal where a lock sealed it from the river. The other feature which set it aside from ordinary canals is that instead of using locks to change the water level, Green used an inclined plane. His tubs were fitted with wheels. At the plane, they were attached to a rope and hauled up the slope to the higher level.

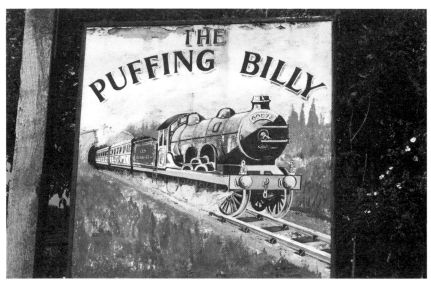

The sign outside The Puffing Billy, Torrington carries artistic licence to its limits. Even the engine's number was a 1948 allocation to former LNER locos, arch rivals of the GWR. (photo: Elizabeth Fowler).

Lime kilns were built at several places along the canal and trade flourished for a while. Coal and limestone travelled inland, agricultural produce and ball clay for the pottery industry in the north midlands was shipped back down to Bideford. Within forty years, railways were perceived as a much more efficient option, and the canal was closed, allowing the railway to build on much of the route – the only possible way up this sheer sided valley.

Railways in the area

The London and South Western Railway opened for business in 1871 and ran to Torrington. Then, in 1888 the Marland Light Railway was opened. It was built by the North Devon Clay Company as a 3ft gauge line to carry their products the six or so miles to Great Torrington, where it was trans-shipped into standard gauge wagons for onward movement. There were several attempts to extend the standard gauge beyond Torrington, all of which foundered until The North Devon and Cornwall Junction Railway Company was formed. They planned to link Torrington with Halwill Junction, where it would meet lines from Bude, Launceston and Okehampton, using the existing narrow gauge track bed. Raising the necessary finance was a major problem, but the chairman Col. H.F. Stephens convinced government that they should invest some cash. This was just after the Great War, and unemployment was intense.

Local authorities then contributed, an Act was obtained, and the first sod was cut on June 30th 1922 by Arthur Neal, Minister of Transport. The Opening Ceremony of the 20½ mile line was performed on July 27th 1925. It was never very well used, running though such a sparsely populated area, and passenger services between Torrington and Halwill were withdrawn on March 1st 1965, with the line still short of its 40th birthday. Clay traffic sustained it between Barnstaple and Meeth until September 13th 1982, and when that finished the line was completely closed.

Frithelstock Priory [3]

This was an Augustinian order founded by Robert de Bello around 1220, and was originally occupied by monks from Hartland Abbey, to the north west (see Walk 24). The ruins are well worth an exploration, as is the parish church alongside. St. Mary and St. Gregory was believed to have been built around the same time as the Priory. It was sited alongside the priory church, the east end of the latter actually touched the south tower of the parish church.

Tarka The Otter

Henry Williamson's closely observed nature story was first published in 1927. A delightful piece of fiction, it was based on Williamson's observations of the otter, then common in north Devon. Much of the landscape he described is unchanged today; particularly the area of Tarka's birth. Both he and his mother swam and caught fish around the Canal Bridge. This is Beam Aqueduct [5]. Many other locations described in those magical pages are easily identifiable locally.

The Walk

To the right-hand side, behind the pub is The Tarka Trail (see Walk 11). Join this turning right, under the road bridge. Note a further arch on the left. This was used by a narrow gauge railway which ran down the valley from the Peters Marland area with clay (see Walk 16), connecting with the London and South Western Railway at their terminus here. Follow the Tarka Trail over the river [1] to the first road crossing up a delightfully wooded valley with a winding stream. Wildlife abounds here. There are masses of birds including long tailed tits, and mammals such as the otter – although you will need to be extremely fortunate to see one. The only evidence usually available to confirm their existence are paw-prints and spraints.

At the road crossing, by an old station platform (Watergate Halt) [2], turn right up the road for a few yards to the Public Footpath sign on the right. Follow this path, up a rather steep hill into Priestacott Farm. Note some of the old car remains here; hardly identifiable, but clearly of considerable vintage. Follow the lane around to the right, and turn left just before the next building, unusually, a dentist's surgery. Round the back, the path leads over the field down into Frithelstock. On meeting the road, turn right, and after a hundred yards, another path leads off to the left. Detour 200 yard along the road here to visit Frithelstock Priory, with The Clinton Arms opposite.

Ahead is a gate in the corner of a field. The path is through this gate, and alongside the left edge of the field. Over a small stream – tricky in wet weather – and up the gentle slope to another road. Turn left. Two hundred yards along, the next footpath sign you need is on the right. This leads over the hill, through another field and into the village of Monkleigh; turn left. At the top of the road, turn right to head downhill. For the pub, and a garage which sells basic refreshment, make a slight detour left here. The walk follows the lane into the Torridge valley, eventually reaching the main road. To the left of the junction is a car park [4] with an underpass leading back to The Tarka Trail. This was first the canal bed, then a railway, and now, back to foot use.

Turn right. After half a mile, note the impressive stone bridge on the right. That is actually Beam Aqueduct [5] that took the canal from one side of the valley to the other, and is now a private drive. A detailed inscription on a stone in the parapet describes the construction, opening, and funding of the canal. Further lengths of the canal are visible in the final few hundred yards of the walk just before you reach the station. Now you can sample the "Scrumpy Jack": if you are not driving. Otherwise, be warned. Phew!!

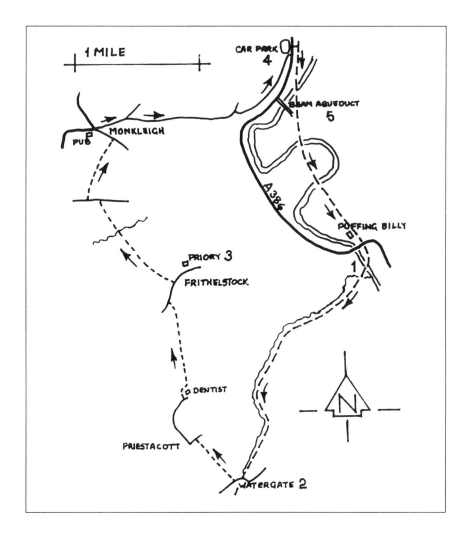

Walk 21:
Taddiport – Torrington Common – Rosemoor

A essentially sub-urban walk packed with interest, offering plenty of "green" without ever getting too far away from the town.

Distance: 5½ miles. With Rosemoor RHS – 6¼ miles.

Terrain: 1 steady climb.

Refreshment: Old Bowling Green Car Park usually has Alberts Chuck Wagon for snacks and Hockings Ice Cream. Try one with Devon cream on top: superb, but about 1m calories!! A shop in Taddiport. The Puffing Billy pub after about 1m (see walk 20), Dartington Glass – if you visit, and Rosemoor (ditto). The latter is something between a tearoom and a restaurant with high quality home-made freshly cooked food, prepared under the watchful eye of proprietor Caroline King. Highly recommended.

Map: 180.

Grid Reference: SS 488188.

Starting Point: The Torridge Inn, Taddiport. In the river valley on the B3227, half a mile south of the A386 Bideford to Great Torrington road.

Transport: Buses to Exeter, Plymouth, Okehampton, Bideford and Barnstaple from Torrington. Torrington only from Taddiport.

The 16th century Torridge Inn has a thatched roof – *de rigeur* in these parts, is built of traditional Devon cob, and was once known as the Canal Tavern. This referred to the time when the Rolle Canal came through here (see Walk 20). A free house, and whilst not so strong(!) on real ales, it does offer best mild, unusual in this part of England. Whitbread, Flowers and Boddingtons are all on tap. It's very much a "local", open all day, with bar snacks always available.

Torrington Commons [3]

These cover 365 acres, with over 20 miles of footpaths. They were originally given by the local Baron FitzRobert "for relief of the poor," and are now jealously guarded by The Commons Conservators; a wonderful part of this town.

Town Mills, Torrington. The Rolle Canal once passed the front door. (photo: Elizabeth Fowler).

Royal Horticultural Society Gardens – Rosemoor [7]

Donated to the RHS in 1988 by Lady Ann Berry these 8 acres of garden were already famed for roses. Now with the resources of the RHS, several exciting developments have already taken place. In its formal gardens are 2,000 roses in 200 different varieties. A Colour Theme Garden, Herb Garden and Potager and a Bog Garden with ornamental lake. Most recent additions are a Cottage Garden and a Foliage Garden, with more planned. Changes and improvements are continuous here, and a hard core of regular visitors return year after year to soak up the glory of the place. Remains of The Rolle Canal run through the grounds

Dartington Crystal [4]

Makers of superb quality glassware, the factory was established in the 1960s by the Dartington Hall Trust with the aim of providing employment and teaching skills in rural areas suffering depopulation. There is a factory tour during working hours where a gallery over the production area gives an excellent view of glassblowers at work. The shop is pure temptation to anyone with even the slightest appreciation of quality and beauty.

Great Torrington Railway [6]

A delightful 7¼" gauge steam railway owned and operated by Roy Foster. Roy moved here in the late 1980s having bought a house with land attached for the prime purpose of indulging his lifelong love of miniature railways. He laid all the track and built the station and engine shed. It is noteworthy for the steep gradients as the line runs up alongside the river. Far more than a "toy train" this is model engineering at its finest. You don't need kids as an excuse to try it. And Roy will always talk about steam in its myriad manifestations.

The Walk

Cross the ancient river bridge [1], noting the old Toll house guarding the crossing, and bear to the right, past Taddiport Chantry Church. This looks almost too small to be a church with its squat building, slate roof and tiny tower, but has a certain appeal. After some 200 yards, take the track which leads off to the right. This follows the river but always looking down to the water. Here, pause a moment and look over your right shoulder for a full view of Taddiport bridge.

Follow the track as it veers left around Servise Farm and cross the old railway carrying Walk 20. After a footbridge over the stream, turn right following the bridleway to the road. Turn right, but note the signpost across the road. It points to: Torrington Station ½m. Fine, but it closed in 1965!

Walking steeply downhill, this road leads to the busy A386, across the flood plain and bridge towards The Puffing Billy where Walk 20 starts. Cross the road just before to see the old river bridge [2], bypassed, but in a superb state of preservation. After crossing the old railway bridge the road swings right, and on the left is a track between the signs that state "Torrington" and "Torrington Common Conservators". This runs alongside but above the road and was once the main road, thankfully unused by traffic now.

At the top of the hill is the Old Bowling Green with toilets and refreshments. Turn left, away from the main road and walk alongside the wall until you reach the first track to the right. Take this, alongside the rear of the cemetery. A sharp left and right brings the walk to the bottom of Stoneman's Lane. On the left, a Public Footpath gives access to Dartington Crystal [4] if you wish to visit. Otherwise, walk down to the next junction.

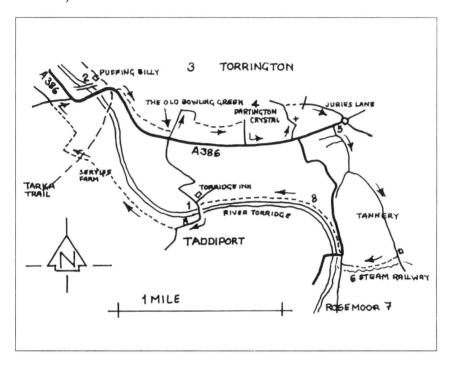

On reaching the main road, turn left. There are several shops, a pub and St. Michael's church, and the streets across gives access to the centre of the town. On reaching Gas Lane, turn left and keep to the left of the Catholic Church of All Saints. The path swings to the left, and then to the right. Turn right on an unmarked and unmade track as the surfaced road goes left again. This leads into Juries lane and back to the main road. Turn right.

Take the first left into East Street [5] and first left again down an unmade road which rapidly narrows into a footpath. Go straight across when the next footpath intersects, and on reaching a road, straight on again down Caddywell Lane with a school to the right. There is an "S" bend along this lane. Look at the building on the right with a rounded corner. That was a tannery before it was so tastefully renovated. Down a steep hill and at the bottom, just before a small bridge is Shallowford House on the left. Turn right through a gate marked Public Footpath, and Entrance to Steam Railway.

More downhill as the track passes the delightful Great Torrington Railway [6]. At the end of the drive, turn left for Rosemoor [7]. The entrance is 200 yards up this road on the right, and walk back the same way after your visit. If you insist upon giving it a miss, turn right towards the road junction. The building across the road was the old Town Mill and evidence of its former use can be seen over the wall. This was re-located here from Taddiport when the Rolle Canal was constructed.

Take the main road towards Torrington, and on the left, after a few yards, a slope leads down towards the river. This is the infilled bed of the Rolle Canal [8], which leads back to Taddiport and the start of the walk. At the far end, note on the right the remains of old lime kilns. This was one of the spots where limestone, carried up the canal was burnt and distributed to farmers.

Walk 22:
Parkham – Nethercott – Melbury Hill – Cabbacott

This is the corner of Devon visitors never see. It's under 2 miles from the coast as the seagull flies, but it might as well not exist. The reason is the A39 trunk road. Clovelly, Bucks Mill, and all the magic-sounding coastal names are to the north; Parkham to the south. And everyone simply looks north. Good. They leave Parkham to those in the know. Rich rolling countryside, Forestry Commission land, pretty streams and bosky valleys.

Distance: 8½m.

Terrain: Hilly.

Refreshment: Noneaprt from the start/finish.

Map: 190.

Grid Reference: SS 387212.

Starting Point: The Bell Inn, Parkham – 1½m south of A39 Bideford – Bude road at Horns Cross.

Transport: Bideford – Hartland service 318 calls at The Hoops Inn on the main road. A lane leads south past Foxdown Hotel for 1,000 yards, to pick the walk up at the point marked with an asterisk: *

Depending on how you approach, first impressions of the 13th Century Bell are of a delightful thatched country pub, or a ramshackle building with a corrugated iron roof. But inside – which is all that really matters – Bass and Flowers are always available, and one guest beer which can cover a whole lot of "real ale". Service is cheerful, and the only downside are the somewhat restricted opening times: 12noon to 2.30pm and 6.30 to 11. Bar snacks are available.

Parkham

The trouble with trying to write about the history of Parkham, is that there really isn't any. It has been settled for centuries – St James Church has a Norman South doorway dated around 1160 although the rest of the building is mainly 15th Century. Otherwise, as so often happens, the world passes by without ruffling the community feathers. Until the 1970s.

At Parkham, the Bell Inn's pretty thatched roof conceals a rather ugly corrugated iron one to the rear. (photo: Alison Fowler)

Increased mobility has made places like Parkham very vulnerable to development. The population has almost doubled within recent years and, bit by bit, the edges of the village succumb to bulldozer and bricklayer bringing "townies" and their perceptions of life in the country; often at odds with those born and bred there. But the place still retains its rural feel, and should absorb much more development before that is lost forever.

The Walk

Leave the pub and turn right, following the road to Broad Parkham. After 150 yards take the right fork, this time ignoring the Broad Parkham direction, past the church and bear left following this road until it turns sharp left. Ahead is a farm complex with a wide track. Take this, and walk down 100 yards to a gate on the left carrying a Waymark arrow. Pass through the gate and down over the field, heading slightly left to a stile which takes the walk into the next field and a left turn. In the far bottom corner is a gate into the next field. This has a left to right slope, and slightly downhill at the far side is a stile. Turn right into a green lane, and follow this for 200 yards before reaching a left turn with Public Footpath sign which leads along a narrow green lane to a road.

   * – alternative start point: *see "transport" at the start of this walk.*

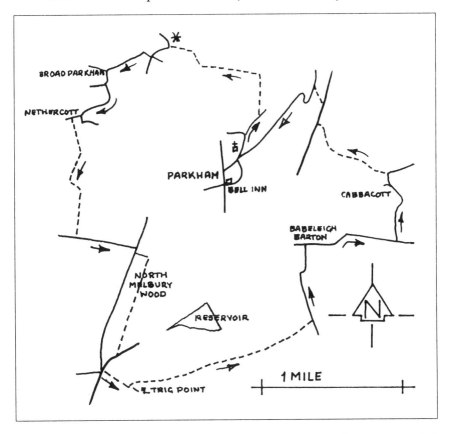

Walk straight ahead for about 300 yards with a very pleasant wooded area on the right until you reach a crossroads. Turn right and follow the lane which moves uphill, along a section overhung with trees, past Broad Parkham Farm and to a three-way junction. Take the fork left towards Bocombe, down into a valley and up the other side to a sharp left-hand bend and a house sign marked "Nethercott". 50 yards beyond, where the lane turns sharp left again, the walk turns right along a track for 100 yards to a gate. Turn left, up a stony lane.

At the next gate, pass through and head slightly to the right towards a gate in the far right corner. Beyond, turn left as soon as the fence allows and follow it to the next gate. Turn left into the lane. When this lane reaches a "T" junction, turn right. Here there is a choice of route. Almost immediately on the left is North Melbury Wood which is mainly conifer, but with some broadleaf species in parts of it. You can turn in there, and after 150 yards follow the track to the right which eventually returns you to a road. Turn right to the next road junction. If you ignore this stroll, walk straight along the road to the next junction.

Together again, across the road is a sweeping entrance to The Forestry Commission's Melbury Hill site. Follow this main driveway until you are almost at the top of the rise where a left fork disappears into the trees, just before a trig point. It's quite wild and unkempt here, but with a wonderful variety of flowers.

The end of woodland sees the walk enter a field. Keep close to the right-hand hedge towards a gate in the opposite corner. To the left as you cross this field, Melbury Reservoir spreads out below. The path continues to hold close to the right-hand edge through the next field, where it picks up a very clear track back to the road. Turn left.

At the "T" junction turn right. Babeleigh Barton is on the left. The Risdon family lived here from the 15th century in what was believed to have been an intriguing series of buildings. These were torn down in 1760, and the current ones have little to commend them architecturally. Follow this lane for almost 1 mile before turning left into yet another valley with a small stream. Climb up the other side, past a huge farm complex at Cabbacott and to a sort of crossroads where the "main" road turns right. Ahead is a sign stating that the road is unsuitable for long vehicles (or any others by the look of it) and the walk takes the left-hand turn. This is steadily downhill in a beautiful green lane.

Where the green lane ends in a gate, a Public Footpath sign points into a wood on the left, down a steep bank, over a stile, and across a couple of wooden planks bridging another stream. Bear to the right, and follow a clearly defined track up the hill and around to the left before meeting another stile. Across, but slightly to the left is a gateway into a field. Take this, and keep close to the left-hand edge until reaching a stile which enters woodland and drops away very steeply to the road. Turn right.

Some 300 yards along on the left, take a green lane which leads to another road. Turn left, steeply uphill and eventually back into Parkham and the pub.

Walk 23:
Beaford – Harepath – Kiverley

One of the less taxing walks in this book, there are no severe hills, just a pleasant stroll through woodland, and one very attractive length beside the river Torridge.

Distance: 4½ miles.

Terrain: Easy, but boggy after rain.

Refreshment: None outside start/finish.

Map: 180.

Grid Reference: SS 553150.

Starting Point: The Globe, Beaford, on the B3220 Torrington to Winkleigh road.

Transport: Red Bus services 75 and 315 link Barnstaple, Bideford and Exeter. Details on 01271 45444.

Frankly, The Globe is not one of the better pubs in this book. It lacks atmosphere, has no real ale, but is still quite an interesting building in its own right. It's a free house, the nearest thing to a good pint being Webster's. But they do have Inch's Cider on draught. Now that is potent. There is no food, and opening hours are restricted and varied by the season.

St. Michael and All Saints Church, Beaford

Architecturally, this church is of no special interest, but the graveyard does hold a curio: or 9 of them. The Trick family have all been buried in identical graves, with full length memorials. Absolutely symmetrical, they date from 1870 to 1915.

The Walk

Leave the pub, turn left towards Winkleigh and cross the road, taking the first right signposted "Merton". Once, there was a pub in the building on this corner called The Gunsmiths, but it has been gone for many years. Some 200 yards along, take a left marked "Rye Park", which leads through Rye Park Close to a stile with a Public Footpath signpost.

This leads through a further 2 fields before reaching a stile that drops the walk into a lane. Take the stile opposite and head diagonally right towards another lane, the entry to which is controlled by a stark granite-posted cattle crush. North Harepath Farm is on the right as the walk turns left.

A delightful wrought iron farm sign, harking back to the days when travellers meant sales representatives, not the less pleasant connotation. (photo: Elizabeth Fowler).

At the top of this lane turn right and follow the road until it starts a descent into the Torridge valley. At the point where it swings sharp left, there is a gate ahead which gives access to a track. After 3 gates, the track itself turns left, but the walk continues straight down the hill to a coppice by the river. Turn right and pick up the path along the bank.

This eventually veers away from the water and moves uphill to join a lane. Turn left, down the hill, and before the river bridge is a gate to the right marked "Public Bridleway". Through this gate is a split in the path: take the one that leads straight ahead. Before long, this becomes met-alled, eventually leading to a lane. Turn right, and after a few yards, take the Public Footpath through a gate on the left. Cross the next stile, keeping close to the left-hand fence. After a few yards, this turns sharp left leaving no clear path. Aim slightly to the left, and down the hill in the valley is a gate beyond which lies Cherry Tree Cottage and a lane. Turn right.

The state of this lane gives a vivid indication of how thin is the veneer of modern roadbuilding. For many lengths, the skim of road surfacing material has broken away revealing original packed earth and stone: a green lane. It also shows graphically that this road has only been treated once since Devon County Council took over maintenance. And because of its narrowness, the centre is a haven for grass, dandelions, and anything else that flourishes with a minimum of sustenance.

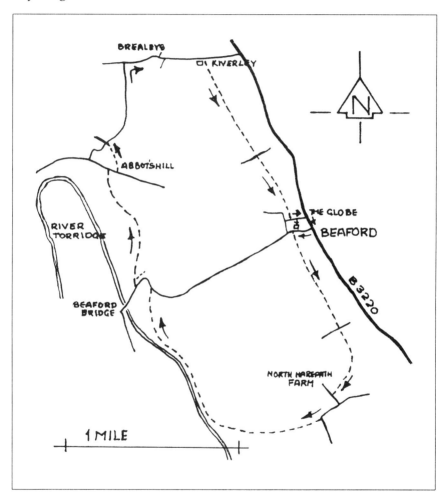

Follow this lane up the gently rising gradient, around the right-hand bend for half a mile, past a farm on the right. Beyond the buildings, a footpath sign points to the right. At the end of this field are 2 gates; aim for the right-hand one. Beyond, keep to the left hedgerow as the next gate is in the far left corner. This leads into a green lane with an exit stile directly opposite. Walk straight across this field. As you come over the rise, a cream painted thatched cottage can be seen. The exit stile is close by this. Pass a barn, turn left, and after a few yards, an iron gate gives access to St. George and All Saints Church. Keeping to the left of the church, a gate leads to the main road, a left turn, and the pub.

Walk 24:
Hartland Quay – Stoke – Spekes Mill

This is a further chance to use some of the South West Coastal Path, combining rugged coastline with gentle inland valleys.

Distance: 5½ miles.

Terrain: 2 steep climbs.

Refreshment: Docton Mill, but irregularly.

Map: 190.

Grid Reference: SS 225248.

Starting Point: The Hartland Quay Hotel. This lies 2½ miles west of Hartland village beyond Stoke. Leave the A39 Bideford to Bude road at Hartland Cross.

Transport: Nothing. Hartland, 2½m away is nearest.

The pub offers superb vistas, and tables outside at which to enjoy your drink; laced with a little salt from the waves which ceaselessly batter the cliffs. In addition to food, there is accommodation on offer, and the place is alive with visitors in the season and during winter weekends when the weather is fine. Those crowds congregate at the pub, and tend not to drift very far, so what might appear to be a very crowded walk will soon settle down into a pleasant quiet one.

Hartland Quay

Strange though it may seem, looking down on the boiling waves, there was once a thriving port here. It was built as the result of an Act of Parliament in 1566 and its Petitioners included some of our greatest naval names: Drake and Raleigh amongst them. It served the local community until finally succumbing to the tempestuous sea in 1896. Before then, its *raison d'etre* had diminished with the improvement of roads in the area, although railways never reached this coast. Hartland once had a dubious claim to fame in that it was the farthest village in England from a railway station. Through the harbour limestone and coal arrived, and agricultural produce shipped out. The current hotel and museum were originally built as Harbourmaster's house, stables and warehouses before conversion.

Hartland Abbey (2) and St Nectans Church (1)

The religious institutions in this area have a somewhat intertwined history. The church was named after a Welsh saint who arrived in the 7th century. He was waylaid at nearby Newton by local ne'er-do-wells and murdered; by decapitation. Undaunted, our saint picked his head up, carried it back to a cave where he lived and placed it on a rock. This is supposed to have retained the mark of the head ever since. A chapel was built upon the spot and his remains preserved there, to be moved only in 1350 when St. Nectans church was built in Stoke.

The good man's influence was reputed to have extended to the mother of King Harold; Gytha (or Gydda). She was a Danish princess, closely related to King Canute, who married the great Saxon patriot Godwin in 1019. It was over four centuries after Nectan's murder that her Godwin was saved in a shipwreck locally. In thanks for this singular deliverance, she founded a collegiate of secular canons at Stoke. Her other contribution to the royal life of this country was to have a daughter, Edith, who married Edward the Confessor.

During the reign of the first Plantaganet Henry II in around 1157, the abbey was established. The abbey church was demolished in the sixteenth century and its work transferred to St. Nectans. The abbey lasted longer than any other in the country, being finally dissolved in 1539 and given by Henry VIII to the sergeant of his wine cellar, William Abbott.

The house passed into private hands and progressively deteriorated until 1779 when the then owner built a new one alongside using some materials from the old building. A further rebuilding took place in 1860, which remains to this day. The collection of documents and early photographs is extensive. Still used as a family home, it is open to visitors: details of times from The Administrator – 0237 441264.

St. Nectans church is well worth exploration. The tower, at 128ft, is the tallest in north Devon and is visible from the sea by sailors. This was used as a point of reference by old navigators. It holds a peal of six bells and can be seen from much of this walk, Inside, the Popes Chamber, over the north porch, contains a small museum of fascinating local relics, including the village stocks, whilst the font was originally installed in the abbey and is believed to be over eight hundred years old.

The 124ft tower of St. Nectans church, Stoke. (photo: Alison Fowler).

Long Peak Rocks ·

The cliffs along which much of this walk passes have long been a graveyard for shipping. Many hundreds of seamen's lives have been lost upon this inhospitable coast. One scene of great heroics involved the Appledore lifeboat (see Walk 18) near Long Peak Rocks. It was a dark and stormy night in November 1962 that the *Green Ranger*, a fleet auxiliary tanker, en-route from Plymouth to Cardiff broke her towline and was driven onto the rocks. The Appledore boat was summoned and her crew showed immense skill and daring saving the men aboard the stricken ship.

Shipwrecks have been a fact of life on this coast for as long as men have sailed. Wreckers were endemic. One story has it that a donkey used to be walked along the cliff edge with a light tied to its tail. The captain of a ship would assume it was another boat in clear safe water and that it was safe for him . . . Even after navigation became a more exact science boats would founder here. Whenever they did, they were stripped of anything of value so quickly that the authorities used to be staggered. The local thinking was "If we don't get it quick, the sea'll have it". Quite reasonable too.

The Walk

The Coastal Path is a few yards above the level of the pub, so set off by walking back up the road to the signposts. Turn left, heading north. The path looks out to sea on the left, and there is often evidence of shipping entering or leaving the Bristol Channel, heading for one of the many ports on both the English and Welsh sides. A ruined tower marks the start of the first of many descents as the path drops down into a valley. Just before the stream, turn right, away from the coast heading inland. Follow the marked path up a hillside and towards the church. Take time to admire the wide range of native English trees along this valley, some with trunks wildly deformed by the passage of time and gales.

This path leads to a road. On reaching it turn left towards the church (1). Pass it, and around the corner the road makes a left and then a right turn into the village of Stoke. Just beyond the right turn is a sort of crossroads with a gap between houses on the right. Take this track, heading south. Go straight on at the next crossroads, but note that the hamlet of Newton is close by on the left, with St. Leonard a little further along. These are places relevant to the legend of St. Nectan.

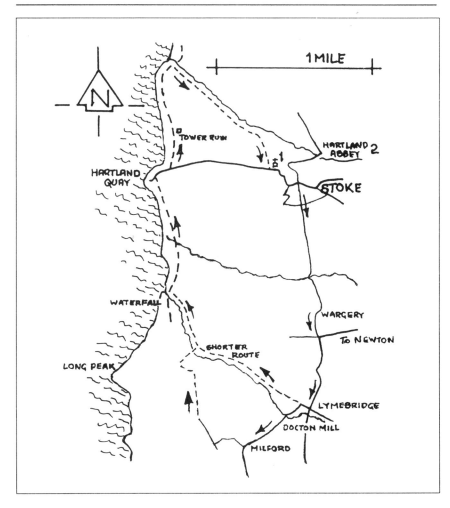

The lane is now a typical Devonian affair with a steep bank at either side and the field beyond. This allows only an occasional view over the landscape which is unfortunate, but does not last for long. The road drops down a steep hill to Lymebridge and a road junction; turn right signposted "Docton Mill" alongside a pretty stream. The mill is a few yards down on the left, and is well worth time spent there. There is also a tea room open during the summer, and the gardens and mill itself are very attractive. It is possible to shorten the walk by about 500 yards here by leaving the road just before it turns left to cross the stream and walking down this path to the sea. But you miss a splendid view.

The walk proper continues up the hill beyond the mill taking the second Public Footpath on the right. This leads eventually to yet another steep downhill slope. Pause at the head of this and take in the glorious panorama before you. Drop down the slope towards a bridge over the stream. Here you meet up with the short cut. At the end is an open area where the walk again meets the Coastal Path. The stream meanwhile has been hurrying towards the Atlantic Ocean. Here, it plunges over a rock face in a spectacular waterfall as it enters the sea: really dramatic. Long Peak faces out to sea just to the left.

Turn right (north), and climb up the steps out of this valley, over the top and down into the next one. The path is clearly marked across the floor of this one which passes over some earthworks and round the back of a sheer (un-named) outcrop. After another climb, the rooftops of Hartland Quay come into view. Take one of the paths back down to the pub.

Walk 25:
Darracott – Gooseham Mill – Mead

For this last walk a little cheating is necessary; but only a little. For a couple of hundred yards, the path strays into Cornwall. There are no distractions or counter-attractons, virtually no housing, and nothing of historical note. But it's super scenery, deliciously remote and a fitting way to take our leave of this glorious part of England.

Distance: 5¼ miles.

Terrain: 2 steep hills including 1 flight of steps.

Refreshment: At the start/finish only.

Map: 190.

Grid Reference: SS 232179.

Starting Point: The Old Smithy Inn, Darracott, off the A39 Bideford to Bude road at Welcombe Cross. An unofficial sign roadside points the way.

Transport: Nothing.

The 13th century thatched pub is, as can be expected, a free house. This often means better beer and better service, and such is the case here. Butcombe bitter is the favourite tipple, and a very good one too, along with varieties of "sleepy juice", also known as cider. Delicious it may be, but remember its soporific effect.

The Walk

Turn left outside the pub and walk up the road for a few hundred yards to a sort of crossroads. A Public Footpath sign to the right indicates the walk. This path soon narrows and starts its downhill plunge towards the valley bottom. There, it joins a wider track before arriving at a pretty stone bridge which takes the path over Marsland Water, a chuckling brook almost at the end of its journey to the Atlantic Ocean. This is the county line: hello Cornwall.

Past some outhouses, the track becomes paved and starts uphill before taking a sharp left-hander. Ahead are two gates. Take the right-hand one, which carries the names "Tall Trees" and "Rosemarsland", but no indication that is it a Public Footpath. Follow that road around to the right, over the sleeper bridge – goodbye Cornwall – and ahead is the gateway to "Tall Trees". To the left, hard by the boundary fence, a signpost directs you to the left.

The Old Smithy Inn at Darracot. (photo: Elizabeth Fowler).

Climb the bosky hillside to a stile into a road at Mead Cross; turn left. This is National Trust land known as Aller Park. Ahead a gate bars the way, but a stile to the left gives access. A sign on the gate informs that this is a footpath only to West Mill. Follow this road downhill towards the lush green valley below. The hillside is covered with shrubs and trees, the latter blown into grotesque shapes by the continual battering of westerly winds off the Atlantic.

West Mill hoves into view, a lovely house snuggling in the valley bottom close to, but built up from, the river. At the entrance, a signpost to the right indicates the direction of the walk, now ever closer to the sea. Then another path joins from the left. This is the South West Coastal Footpath and time to climb out of the valley heading north. One of the steepest climbs in the book is not helped by the fact that much of it is in the form of somewhat iregular steps cut into the hillside.

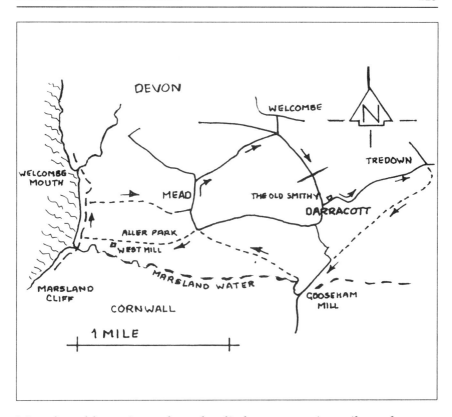

Many breathless minutes later the climb peters out in a stile; perhaps an opportune time to pause, get a second wind, and admire the view out over the Atlantic. This is due west, and nothing but 3,000 miles of ocean until the North American continent. The next turn is not signposted, but is just over the brow of this hill, before a stile and the start of the next descent. Another stile on the right gives access to a field heading away from the sea.

This leads to a road and the settlement of Mead. Turn left. Two hundred yards along, turn right into another narrow country lane and follow this down a hill – not so steep this time – and to a road junction. Take the right-hand road, with an unofficial direction sign to the pub. At the end of this road, turn left and the pub is just around the corner. Now you can risk indulging in the cider.

We publish guides to individual towns, plus books on walking and cycling in the great out-doors throughout England and Wales. This is a recent selection:

More Books about the South-West

EXPLORE THE COAST OF DEVON – Paul Wreyford *(£6.95)*

MYTHS AND LEGENDS OF CORNWALL – Craig Weatherhill & Paul Devereux *(£6.95)*

CORNISH PLACE NAMES & LANGUAGE – Craig Weatherhill *(£6.95)*

PUB WALKS IN SOUTH DEVON – Laurence Main *(£6.95)*

PUB WALKS ON DARTMOOR – Laurence Main *(£6.95)*

PUB WALKS IN CORNWALL – Laurebce Main *(£6.95)*

PUB WALKS ON EXMOOR – Philip Pond *(£6.95)*

CYCLING IN THE WEST COUNTRY – Helen Stephenson *(£7.95)*

Other Destinations

FIFTY CLASSIC WALKS IN THE PENNINES – Terry Marsh *(£8.95)*

WEST PENNINE WALKS – Mike Cresswell *(£5.95)*

HILL WALKS IN MID WALES – Dave Ing *(£8.95)*

WELSH WALKS: Dolgellau /Cambrian Coast – L. Main & M. Perrott *(£5.95)*

WELSH WALKS: Aberystwyth & District – L. Main & M. Perrott *(£5.95)*

WALKS IN MYSTERIOUS WALES – Laurence Main *(£7.95)*

RAMBLES IN NORTH WALES – Roger Redfern *(£6.95)*

RAMBLES AROUND MANCHESTER – Mike Cresswell *(£5.95)*

EAST CHESHIRE WALKS – Graham Beech *(£5.95)*

TEA SHOP WALKS IN THE CHILTERNS – Jean Patefield *(£6.95)*

BY-WAY BIKING IN THE CHILTERNS – Henry Tindell *(£7.95)*

PUB WALKS IN SNOWDONIA – Laurence Main *(£6.95)*

BEST PUB WALKS AROUND CHESTER & THE DEE VALLEY – John Haywood *(£6.95)*

BEST PUB WALKS IN GWENT – Les Lumsdon *(£6.95)*

PUB WALKS IN POWYS – Les Lumsdon & Chris Rushton *(£6.95)*

BEST PUB WALKS IN PEMBROKESHIRE – Laurence Main *(£6.95)*

BEST PUB WALKS AROUND CENTRAL LONDON – Ruth Herman *(£6.95)*

BEST PUB WALKS IN ESSEX – Derek Keeble *(£6.95)*

More Pub Walks . . .

There are many more titles in our fabulous series of 'Pub Walks' books for just about every popular walking area in the UK, all featuring access by public transport. We label our more recent ones as 'best' to differentiate them from inferior competitors!

Explore the Lake District:

THE LAKELAND SUMMITS – Tim Synge *(£7.95)*

100 LAKE DISTRICT HILL WALKS – Gordon Brown *(£7.95)*

LAKELAND ROCKY RAMBLES: Geology beneath your feet – Brian Lynas *(£7.95)*

FULL DAYS ON THE LAKELAND FELLS: Challenging Walks – Adrian Dixon *(£7.95)*

PUB WALKS IN THE LAKE DISTRICT – Neil Coates *(£6.95)*

LAKELAND WALKING, ON THE LEVEL – Norman Buckley *(£6.95)*

MOSTLY DOWNHILL: LEISURELY WALKS, LAKE DISTRICT – Alan Pears *(£6.95)*

Cycling . . .

CYCLE UK! The essential guide to leisure cycling – Les Lumsdon *(£9.95)*

OFF-BEAT CYCLING IN THE PEAK DISTRICT – Clive Smith *(£6.95)*

MORE OFF-BEAT CYCLING IN THE PEAK DISTRICT – Clive Smith *(£6.95)*

50 BEST CYCLE RIDES IN CHESHIRE – edited by Graham Beech *(£7.95)*

CYCLING IN THE COTSWOLDS – Stephen Hill *(£6.95)*

CYCLING IN THE CHILTERNS – Henry Tindell *(£7.95)*

CYCLING IN THE LAKE DISTRICT – John Wood *(£7.95)*

CYCLING IN LINCOLNSHIRE – Penny & Bill Howe *(£7.95)*

CYCLING IN NOTTINGHAMSHIRE – Penny & Bill Howe *(£7.95)*

CYCLING IN STAFFORDSHIRE – Linda Wain *(£7.95)*

CYCLING IN THE WEST COUNTRY – Helen Stephenson *(£7.95)*

CYCLING IN SOUTH WALES – Rosemary Evans *(£7.95)*

CYCLING IN NORTH WALES – Philip Routledge *(£7.95) ... available 1996*

Sport . . .

RED FEVER: from Rochdale to Rio as 'United' supporters – Steve Donoghue *(£7.95)*

UNITED WE STOOD: unofficial history of the Ferguson years – Richard Kurt *(£6.95)*

MANCHESTER CITY: Moments to Remember – John Creighton *(£9.95)*

- plus many more entertaining and educational books being regularly added to our list. All of our books are available from your local bookshop. In case of difficulty, or to obtain our complete catalogue, please contact:

Sigma Leisure, 1 South Oak Lane, Wilmslow, Cheshire SK9 6AR
Phone: 01625 – 531035   Fax: 01625 – 536800

ACCESS and VISA orders welcome – call our friendly sales staff or use our 24 hour Answerphone service! Most orders are despatched on the day we receive your order – you could be enjoying our books in just a couple of days. Please add £2 p&p to all orders.